M000045102

Salvation LIFE BOOKS

Spiritual Formation

Wesleyan Perspective

SalvationLife.com

Four Weeks of Preparing the Soul for Christmas

WAIT

Daniel Ethan Harris

Salvation
LIFE
BOOKS

SalvationLife Books
www.salvationlife.com/books
E-mail: daniel@salvationlife.com

Copyright © 2014 Daniel Ethan Harris

All rights reserved. No part of this book may be reproduced in any form without written permission from SalvationLife Books.

ISBN-10: 0692291539
ISBN-13: 978-0692291535

Cover design: Roy Migabon: roymigabon.weebly.com
Cover image: Oleg Mikhaylov/Shutterstock

Unless otherwise noted, Scripture quotations are from *New Revised Standard Version Bible*, copyright 1989, Division of Christian Education of the National Council of the Churches of Christ in the United States of America. Used by permission. All rights reserved.

When noted as "NIV," Scripture quotations are from *THE HOLY BIBLE, NEW INTERNATIONAL VERSION®*, NIV® Copyright © 1973, 1978, 1984, 2011 by Biblica, Inc.® Used by permission. All rights reserved worldwide.

Prayers are from *The Book of Common Prayer of the Episcopal Church*, New York: Oxford University Press, 1979.

Revised Common Lectionary copyright 1992, Consultation on Common Texts. Used by permission.

For my mother, Cathy Harris.
One day, the waiting will be over.

Contents

Preface

A NUMBER OF YEARS AGO, the church I attend set up a very nice nativity set in the front of our sanctuary during the four weeks leading up to Christmas, when we observe Advent. The figurines were large and well-made, ready to take their part in the church's celebration of Christmas. The wise men, shepherds, livestock, angels, Joseph, and Mary had all taken their places for the festivities, but we were missing one notable character: there was no baby Jesus. The hay-laden manger had an indentation where the infant figurine was supposed to be, but his absence was glaring.

The stance of the Virgin Mary figurine, which normally looked peaceful and worshipful in adoration of her infant son, was translated into desperation as she held one hand out toward the makeshift cradle and the other over her heart, as if the baby had vanished and left her suddenly unable to breathe. Joseph looked resolute, with lantern and staff already in hand, intent on recruiting a search party from among the magi and shepherds, ready to mount the ox, horse, and donkey, and dash out to look for the boy.

For four consecutive Sundays, I walked past that nativity set and looked at the empty feeding trough where I expected to find the Christ-figurine. Then finally, late on Christmas Eve, our family went with so many others to light our candles, sing the familiar Christmas hymns, and celebrate his birth, and there he was—right in the miniature manger where I had looked for him during the previous month. Mary, Joseph, and the search party suddenly looked much more relaxed. Christmas had come.

An unexpected result of the Jesus-figurine's four-week absence from his place in the nativity was that I paid a significantly higher amount of attention to him and his place in that scene than I would have if he'd been there all along. If you pause long enough to think about it, perhaps you want that same result of increased attention to the newborn king this year, too. Whether or not you are part of a church that observes the season of Advent, the lesson applies, and this book will explore it.

————

This book originated as a series of daily Advent emails I created for my church, First United Methodist Church of Midland, Texas. Since the goal of that series was to help people read and pray throughout Advent, I have kept the daily and weekly prayers that were part of the email series, which are taken from *The Book of Common Prayer*. I am deeply grateful for the encouragement of my pastors and friends in my church.

I greatly value the feedback and editing help from Ryan Bash, Emily Bosland, Robert Pelfrey, and my wife, Kara.

My deepest gratitude goes to Kara, Ethan, and Mia. The love we share in our home is the greatest joy of my life.

Wait

WHAT WOULD IT BE LIKE to awaken on Christmas morning and feel like your soul has been sufficiently prepared to celebrate the incarnation of the Son of God?

I can't say I know what that feels like yet. I've been better prepared some years than others, but overall, I've experienced the opposite of that well-preparedness too many times. Once most Christmases have come and gone, even though I've been mindful that an inescapable reminder of Jesus' birth is at the core of all of the hubbub, I've still had a sense that I missed the point of it all. More than once, I've felt like all of the parties, presents, decorations, movies, and cookies have ended up feeling like hosting a celebration for someone and then forgetting to ever speak to the honoree at the actual event. Sometime during the week between Christmas and New Year's Day, I end up wanting to utter a prayer along the lines of, "Sorry I missed you at the party we threw for you last week." I have realized that if go about my preparation in the same way as usual, I will end up needing to say that prayer again.

I want this year to be different. By the time that we sing "Silent Night" in church on Christmas Eve, I want to be able to let the events of that holy night take their full intended effect upon how I choose to live each day. I want to look at my preschool-age children differently and marvel at the fact that God saw it fit to become one of them. I want to be attentive to

God and those around me, staying calm and quiet enough to be able to block out the excess noise and distractions in order to love well anyone with whom I come into contact.

I guess what I want most of all is joy. I can look back at the way I have celebrated Christmas in the past, and while things have been fun, this year I'm less interested in more of the same and more interested in cultivating joy, a pervasive sense of well-being[1], because of the fact that the Lord has come and he indeed does rule the world with truth and grace.

I want to be better prepared for Christmas this year, but according to Christian tradition there's a very counter-cultural irony here: *we will be better prepared for the Christmas season if we have the discipline to wait until it arrives,* and it isn't here yet. It will be an aid to anyone's faith to realize that there is another way of marking time. We've been given a calendar for the purpose of developing our lives with God, handed down to us by centuries of people who have sought to follow Christ closely. I've come to find this calendar to be a much more trustworthy way of looking at the year than unconsciously judging the beginning and end of Christmas by what happens in the stores and on TV. In contrast to the culture around us (where Christmas items are on display in early October and the season will be over by December 26, at the latest), the traditional Christian calendar insists: *It isn't Christmas yet. It's Advent.*

I believe that the more attention we pay to this other calendar, the better chance we give ourselves to have the kind of deeply good Christmas we really desire. In other words, if I want to sing "Silent Night" and "Joy to the World" for all their worth in church on Christmas Eve, I would be wise to spend the weeks between now and then letting "Come, Thou Long-Expected Jesus" fill my mind.

It may come as a surprise to you, as it did to me several years ago, that according to this traditional Christian way of marking the year, Advent isn't Christmas. Advent *prepares* us for Christmas (all twelve days of it—not just one—from December 25 until January 5), but it does so indirectly. It prepares us by not yet focusing on the angels, shepherds, and the manger in Bethlehem. Instead, our attention is directed toward Israel's past longing for the Messiah to come, Christians' future hope that Christ will come again, and the implications of both of these on how we live today in light of Jesus' teaching that he comes and makes his home in us.

Advent is characterized by words like waiting, longing, standing firm, watching, readiness, and staying awake. It puts us among the centuries of God's people who have cried, "How long, O Lord?" If we can remain in this ready, longing, watchful waiting, we will be prepared to recognize and celebrate Christ's coming.

During the coming weeks, we'll seek to prepare our souls for the joy of Christmas by waiting in expectant anticipation. Tomorrow, we'll look at what it means to wait on God, and how we go about doing so.

A Prayer for the Day:

O God, you make us glad with the weekly remembrance of the glorious resurrection of your Son our Lord: Give us this day such blessing through our worship of you, that the week to come may be spent in your favor; through Jesus Christ our Lord. Amen.

A Prayer for the Week:

Almighty God, give us grace to cast away the works of darkness, and put on the armor of light, now in the time of this mortal life in which your Son Jesus Christ came to visit us in great humility; that in the last day, when he shall come again in his glorious majesty to judge both the living and the dead, we may rise to the life immortal; through him who lives and reigns with you and the Holy Spirit, one God, now and for ever. Amen.

Why Waiting Isn't One of My Specialties

*I **wait** for the LORD, my whole being **waits**,*
and in his word I put my hope.
*I **wait** for the Lord*
more than watchmen wait for the morning,
more than watchmen wait for the morning.
(Psalm 130:5-6, NIV)

SUGGESTING THAT ADVENT IS ABOUT WAITING—that it is a period of time for us to recognize the ways that the people of God have waited on God through the centuries, and for us to follow their lead and wait on God ourselves—is likely to raise our defenses in some ways. In my experience, when people are asked about the kinds of activities they enjoy, I have never heard anyone respond with an answer along the lines of, "One of my favorite hobbies is just…waiting on things." We view waiting as an interruption in our plans of how things should go. Our attitude toward waiting reminds me of a comment from my son when he was about three years old. He was playing with some toys in his room when I asked him to help me clean up some of the clothes he had scattered around on his floor. Without looking up from his toys, he said, "Sorry, that's not one of my specialties."

It's easy for us to react that way when we talk about waiting on God. Better to leave that kind of thing to the professionals, we think. Then, throw into the mix that this series of Advent devotionals has waiting as its theme, and I would be surprised if some of us have not already subconsciously decided that we may keep reading, but probably won't actually do anything that gets suggested as a practice of waiting on God. Ruth Haley Barton observes, "Most of us are not very good at waiting. We want what we want, and we want it yesterday. We want it on our own terms, just like we envisioned it....When there is something we need, having to wait for it puts us in a position where we are not in control....This is a necessary and yet very humbling aspect of ordinary life and of the spiritual life."[2]

I think there's also another reason why eagerness to develop waiting as one of our specialties is a rarity: when we talk about waiting on God, we may initially nod our heads in agreement while at the same time only have a hazy idea of how anyone might actually attempt it. We wonder, what exactly is it that we're supposed to do?

Fortunately, there is a specific, practical answer to that question, and we will spend the remainder of this week exploring it. My hope is that doing so will give each of us a concrete idea of how we could go about waiting on God, and hopefully even make a plan to do so for the rest of Advent. We'll get into some specifics over the next few days, but for now, this question might point us in a helpful direction:

If I were to shape the next twenty-four hours of my life in a way that fosters my love for God and for other people, what would I do?

A Prayer for the Day:

O God, the King eternal, whose light divides the day from the night and turns the shadow of death into the morning: Drive far from us all wrong desires, incline our hearts to keep your law, and guide our feet into the way of peace; that, having done your will with cheerfulness while it was day, we may, when night comes, rejoice to give you thanks; through Jesus Christ our Lord. Amen.

A Prayer for the Week:

Almighty God, give us grace to cast away the works of darkness, and put on the armor of light, now in the time of this mortal life in which your Son Jesus Christ came to visit us in great humility; that in the last day, when he shall come again in his glorious majesty to judge both the living and the dead, we may rise to the life immortal; through him who lives and reigns with you and the Holy Spirit, one God, now and for ever. Amen.

Wait—Pray

*First, all who desire the grace of God are to **wait** for it in the way of prayer.*[3]
- John Wesley

I'VE NOTICED SOMETHING ABOUT PRAYER over the past few years: sometimes we pray because we sincerely want to be in God's will, and at other times we pray because we sincerely want God to be in ours. I've done my share of each of these. There have been times when I have prayed with the deepest intention of being open to God and becoming more completely his. This isn't limited to praying about things going on in my own life, but can certainly include times when I pray for others. Though it isn't always the way we go about it, we can pray for others in a way that holds them before God, asking for his kingdom to come and his will to be done on earth in their lives, just as it is in heaven. Whether for myself or for others, the times when I have prayed in these ways could be described as seeking "God's will: nothing more, nothing less, nothing else."[4]

Then, of course, there have been plenty of other times when my praying has boiled down to trying really hard to convince God to give me something that I wanted (usually followed for a while by a lack of praying, because the request I had been making didn't happen according to my terms). During these times, Richard Foster's words describe my prayer precisely: "Our needs, our wants, our concerns dominate our prayer experience. Our prayers are shot through with plenty of pride, conceit, vanity, pretentiousness, haughtiness, and general all-around egocentricity."[5]

I've heard people say that there is no bad way to pray, and generally I agree. So, despite how the previous paragraphs may appear, I do not mean to communicate that one of these kinds of prayer is good and the other one bad. Foster's point in describing the selfishness of our prayers is that we should lay them out before God without regard to their level of egocentricity, considering that we cannot go around selfish prayer, but that we must go through it in order to lay aside our own wills in favor of God's.

However, in light of the issue we discussed yesterday (that we don't like to wait, because we don't like to give up control), it's important for us to realize that while there may be no bad way to pray, some ways of praying are more helpful than others—particularly when it comes to how our aversion to waiting on God drives us to resist giving control to him. While we should indeed feel free to come to God honestly with our concerns without feeling any need to censor them, if we want to cultivate our ability to wait on God, we will need some practices that help us to intentionally surrender the illusion that we have total control over our lives and instead entrust ourselves to God and his kingdom.

For the remainder of this week, we will look at different practical ways that we can wait on God throughout the rest of Advent. While it may seem counter-intuitive to talk about waiting on God as doing things, much of Christian tradition insists on the wisdom of this approach. Waiting on God requires our intentional cooperation, and it's inevitable that if we don't decide now on some ways to deliberately wait on God between now and Christmas, we will come to December 25th with souls prepared (or ill-prepared) to the same degree as they have been in the past.

So, for today's suggestion of how we might wait on God this Advent through prayer, I pass on a helpful approach from James Bryan Smith's great book, *The Good and Beautiful Life*.

You might want to try this at least once per week throughout the rest of Advent[6]:

- Set aside ten to fifteen minutes.
- Think about all of the things you might be anxious about.
- Write them down in your journal or a notebook.
- Ask what you can do to remedy each of these situations.
- Make a note to yourself to do the things you can do.
- Turn everything else over to God.
- Write your request to God, and be specific.

Much of the point of waiting on God through these kinds of practices is that doing them helps put our lives into contact with God's kingdom. When we pray in this way, we can realize that our actions do not need to be done in our own strength, but that the things that have been worrying us are no threats whatsoever to God's kingdom, and therefore we too can safely entrust ourselves to him.

A Prayer for the Day:

O God, the author of peace and lover of concord, to know you is eternal life and to serve you is perfect freedom: Defend us, your humble servants, in all assaults of our enemies; that we, surely trusting in your defense, may not fear the power of any adversaries; through the might of Jesus Christ our Lord. Amen.

A Prayer for the Week:

Almighty God, give us grace to cast away the works of darkness, and put on the armor of light, now in the time of this mortal life in which your Son Jesus Christ came to visit us in great humility; that in the last day, when he shall come again in his glorious majesty to judge both the living and the dead, we may rise to the life immortal; through him who lives and reigns with you and the Holy Spirit, one God, now and for ever. Amen.

Wait—Read

*Secondly. All who desire the grace of God are to **wait** for it
in searching the Scriptures.*[7]
- John Wesley

MY FIRST SUGGESTION, WHICH I MADE YESTERDAY, on how to wait for God throughout Advent was to do so through prayer. That probably didn't come as a surprise to anyone, and today's suggestion of reading the Scriptures is also unlikely to rock anyone's boat. "Pray and read the Bible" are the standard answers most of us have heard throughout our lives for how to seek God. Yet, as we consider these practices in the context of waiting on God, we might realize that we can do them in ways that either enable us to wait (by relinquishing the tight grip of control we like to attempt to maintain on our own lives) or that work against our skills in waiting (by making us hold on more tightly).

This dynamic may be easier to see when we consider the ways that we pray. Like we discussed yesterday, we often either pray out of a sincere desire to be in God's will, or we pray out of a sincere desire for him to be in ours. Could it be that this issue of who is in control also affects the ways that we read the Bible?

I hope that at some point in your life you will follow one of the many plans available that gives you a schedule for reading through the Bible in a certain period of time. There are plans that take a year, while some take up to three years or are as short as ninety days. A huge benefit of following these plans is an increased awareness of the overarching story of God's work in human history that takes place throughout the entire Bible.

My wife and I were following one of these plans a few years ago and we both benefitted from doing so. However, she made an observation about reading the Bible in that manner which stood out to me: she said that there were repeated times when she was reading a passage and something stood out to her which made her want to spend more time in that passage and go further into its meaning, but she couldn't do so because she needed to keep up with the reading plan rather than pause with that passage and fall behind. This points to something that can be a disadvantage in our normal ways of reading the Bible: they may help us get a better grasp of the information that's there, but they often leave us controlling what happens with God as we read the Bible (or we even relegate that control to "the plan") rather than doing something much more risky: giving up our control and allowing ourselves to be vulnerable to what God my choose to say to us through the Scriptures. Dallas Willard points out this tension when he says that our goal in reading the Scriptures is not to get us all of the way through the Bible, but to get the Bible all of the way through us.[8]

New Testament scholar Robert Mulholland gives us a powerful image for thinking about how we might come to the Scriptures in a way that helps us to wait on God through them.[9] He explores a passage from Hebrews 4, which describes the word of God as "living and active, sharper than any two-edged sword, piercing until it divides soul from spirit, joints from marrow; it is able to judge the thoughts and intentions of the heart." The next verse describes what should be our posture before the word of God: "...before him no creature is hidden, but all are naked and laid bare to the eyes of the one to whom we must render an account."[10]

Mulholland explains that the term translated as "laid bare" is the same word that would have been used for an animal about to have its throat cut to be sacrificed, or for the defeated gladiator laid across the knee of the victor with throat exposed before the death blow. So, according to this, it might help get the point across if the next time you read the Bible, you do so with your head laid back and throat exposed, insisting that God, through the Scriptures, can have his way with you.

How comfortable would *that* make you feel? I don't know about you, but if I think of reading the Bible during Advent, I tend to think of things like singing angels, twinkling stars, and happily expectant mothers. That's a far cry from what many of the Advent readings actually are and how we might go about reading them in a "giving myself over to God in a throat-exposed" kind of way.

In light of this, I'd like to suggest a way of reading the Scriptures for the remainder of Advent. This book's first Appendix lists the traditional Advent readings for each respective week from the Revised Common Lectionary. Here's what I suggest:

- **Read the four passages at least once each day during the week.** This act of reading passages repeatedly points us in the direction of waiting on God through the Scriptures. Whereas normally we shy away from re-reading anything we've read before in favor of moving on, reading this way can open us up to the Bible differently.

- **Notice your reaction to at least one of the readings.** By reading repeatedly, you will likely have some kind of a reaction to at least one of the passages. You may be surprised by it, it may cause some kind of longing in you, or perhaps you'll find yourself being resistant to—or even disliking—something that one of the passages says. Pay attention to this as you read the passages each day.

- Sometime near the end of the week, **spend five to ten minutes asking God what it is about that passage that connects with your life**. It's fine if you don't have any significant insights while doing so (remember—we're attempting to wait on God and give him the control rather than keeping it for ourselves), but it's likely that sometime during Advent, the Lord will lead you. It may be in obvious ways, or it may be in more subtle changes in your thinking, but waiting on God through the Scriptures in this way *will* have a long-term effect on us.

A Prayer for the Day:

Lord God, almighty and everlasting Father, you have brought us in safety to this new day: Preserve us with your mighty power, that we may not fall into sin, nor be overcome by adversity; and in all we do, direct us to the fulfilling of your purpose; through Jesus Christ our Lord. Amen.

A Prayer for the Week:

Almighty God, give us grace to cast away the works of darkness, and put on the armor of light, now in the time of this mortal life in which your Son Jesus Christ came to visit us in great humility; that in the last day, when he shall come again in his glorious majesty to judge both the living and the dead, we may rise to the life immortal; through him who lives and reigns with you and the Holy Spirit, one God, now and for ever. Amen.

Wait—Eat and Drink

*Thirdly. All who desire an increase of the grace of God are to **wait** for it in partaking of the Lord's Supper.[11]*
- John Wesley

I ENJOY SPENDING A GOOD BIT OF MY TIME AND ENERGY helping pastors in different ways and accompanying them in their very difficult work. One of the ways that I enjoy most is assisting a pastor in serving Holy Communion.

When I am one of the people who gets to help distribute the bread and wine or juice to others as together we all seek to take in the body and blood of Christ, I am given a different perspective on what is happening. I get to see more faces, more hands, and more eyes of the people participating alongside me as we take part in this ancient form of following our Messiah. I've seen all kinds of things when I'm on that side of the Lord's Supper.

Some of the things I've seen haven't been pretty. Once, when Communion was being served in the method that pastors call "intinction" (when people are given a piece of bread to dip into juice and then eat), I saw a woman realize that she had begun to eat her bread before the arrival of the cup. Then, in one of those war movie-like ultra-slow-motion moments which I was too far away to stop, she took the bread back out of her mouth and dipped it in the cup while the pastor was already looking ahead at the next person. Lesson learned: I will always watch the person I'm serving, and—if need be—assure them that Jesus doesn't mind if they did things out of order and that another piece of bread is available.

Thankfully, seeing those kinds of things has been extremely rare. Much more often, I see things that aren't particularly important in any way, but just interesting observations. Some people like to fold up their piece of the body of Christ while others prefer it fluffy. Some people chew the bread slowly and others pop it as if it were medicine. When the juice is distributed in small cups for each individual, some people like to wait with their bread until they also have their juice in hand. Then, of course, there are those who look very comfortable with such a small glass and almost attack it, throwing their head back like it's a shot glass.

And even more thankfully, more often than those things, I get to see things that remind me of the holiness of the moment: like when I see an elderly man hobble to the front with his cane, but still insist on kneeling to take Communion; or when I see a line of people waiting for the Lord's Supper, which includes people from across every distinction that gets drawn in the world around us—men and women, different races, young and old, educated and uneducated, rich and poor— each coming to Jesus' table together. Some people's faces express pain, others joy. Some people's hands are rough and mature, others are soft with the large majority of what they will touch in life yet to be discovered. Some people's eyes are young and reveal that they can't possibly fully grasp the significance of what they're about to do with that bread and juice, while other people's are old and also reveal that they can't possibly fully grasp the significance of what they're about to do with that bread and juice. There are many distinctions, but we're all there together, each and every one of us as equally undeserving of the invitation as everyone else.

When we receive that bread and juice, we—in the most physical, concrete way possible—are inviting Jesus Christ to come into the deepest places of who we are. Or, I guess it would be better to say that we're accepting his invitation to be a place where he comes to dwell. Either way, it's worth doing, and worth doing at every opportunity.

I hope that you have the opportunity to receive the Lord's Supper during Advent, because it's one of the best ways we have to wait on him. We do it repeatedly throughout the course of our lives because as he makes his home ever more fully in us, there is always another room in the houses of our souls that he hasn't yet occupied.

But there's another angle to this, which blows my mind: waiting on God by taking the Lord's Supper during Advent is especially appropriate because, as we'll explore next week, one of the themes of Advent is the reminder to live in a constant state of readiness for Jesus' return. We await the new heavens and new earth when the dead will rise to new life and God will finally and fully set everything right—forever—with the One reigning at the center of it all who said, "Do this in remembrance of me."

The Bible tells us precious little about what will happen then, but it repeatedly compares that day to a banquet. To my memory, Jesus only mentioned one thing that he would do with us, after that day when what has happened to him in his resurrection will happen to us and to all of creation—when everything is made new: "I tell you, I will never again drink of this fruit of the vine until that day when I drink it new with you in my Father's kingdom."[12]

The words Jesus said to his disciples just before those are the same words we hear each time we're invited to partake: "Take, eat. This is my body....Drink from this cup, all of you, for this is my blood of the new covenant...." In other words, here's the mind-blowing part: We will receive Jesus' supper again with him in the future, when all things are made new, and every time we receive it in the present is an advance participation in what, one day, we will do together again with him.

So we eat, we drink, and we wait—in remembrance of him.

The Advent suggestion for this practice is simple: receive the Lord's Supper at every opportunity you are given.

A Prayer for the Day:

Heavenly Father, in you we live and move and have our being: We humbly pray you so to guide and govern us by your Holy Spirit, that in all the cares and occupations of our life we may not forget you, but may remember that we are ever walking in your sight; through Jesus Christ our Lord. Amen.

A Prayer for the Week:

Almighty God, give us grace to cast away the works of darkness, and put on the armor of light, now in the time of this mortal life in which your Son Jesus Christ came to visit us in great humility; that in the last day, when he shall come again in his glorious majesty to judge both the living and the dead, we may rise to the life immortal; through him who lives and reigns with you and the Holy Spirit, one God, now and for ever. Amen.

Wait—Quiet

*For God alone my soul **waits** in silence; from him comes my salvation. He alone is my rock and my salvation, my fortress; I shall never be shaken.*
(Psalm 62:1-2)

SO FAR THIS WEEK, we have considered three practical ways of waiting on God, each of which requires action on our part: prayer, reading the Scriptures, and receiving the Lord's Supper. Today, we'll look at another way of waiting that is related to those and further enhances them. Today's way of waiting is perhaps the most radical of any of the practices I'm recommending for Advent, and will likely be the most difficult for many of us. This is ironic because this is the discipline that actually asks the least of us—rather than asking us to wait on God by requiring our *action*, today we'll consider how we might wait on God by our *inaction*.

To be precise, today I am tying together two practices for waiting on God that have been recommended for centuries by those before us who have waited on God: silence and solitude. (Don't panic, extroverts, you'll have your day tomorrow.)

Here's an interesting thing about these two practices (and for the moment we'll focus on solitude): we read about the priority solitude played in the lives of many people in the Scriptures, including Moses, Elijah, John the Baptist, Paul, and Jesus himself. Yet we somehow think that in our day it's a practice that's only useful for monks or contemplative-types who are particularly into "that sort of thing."

Dallas Willard describes this well:

The life alienated from God collapses when deprived of its support from the sin-laden world. But the life in tune with God is actually nurtured by time spent alone. John the Baptist, like many of his forerunners in the prophetic line, was much alone in the deserted places of his land. Jesus constantly sought solitude from the time of his baptism up to the Garden of Gethsemane, when he even went apart from those he took there to watch with him. It is solitude and solitude alone that opens the possibility of a radical relationship to God that can withstand all external events up to and beyond death. [13]

I suspect that the last sentence of the paragraph above identifies the issue for many of us: is the kind of "radical relationship with God" that would include regular practices of silence and solitude really *necessary*? Can't we get by fine without them?

It's possible that you're strong enough to lead the kind of life with God that enlivens your soul and blesses the world through you without practices as drastic as silence and solitude, but I certainly am not. I wither without them. I readily admit that part of the reason for that has to do with my personality, and that these practices are perhaps more necessary for people as introverted as I am than for most people, but I think the issue goes deeper than our personality preferences.

Here's my theory: as a generalization, we have stopped using the life of Jesus and the lives of the great ones of his way as our *practical* standard for how we can live our lives. We look at them, admire them, think about the ideas they talked about, and usually begin to use some of those ideas in our conversations, but we rarely consider the obvious option of taking on their lifestyle—seeking to do the kinds of things they did in order to become the kind of people they were. So, when it comes to Jesus and Paul, or more recent figures such as John Wesley, or even people we have known and loved, we tend to admire them, but we treat them as oddities—eccentric people who were zapped by God with special abilities to go to such great lengths.

Particularly in the case of Jesus, treating him like that may be a form of *admiration*, but it isn't a form of *trust*. It's a way of keeping our lives at a distance from his, a way of associating ourselves with Jesus without giving him control, a way of avoiding waiting on God through a lifestyle like that of Jesus.

According to Willard:

> *Our modern religious context assures us that such drastic action as we see in Jesus and Paul [in their use of practices such as solitude] is not necessary for our Christianity—may not even be useful, may even be harmful....Both the secular and the religious setting in which we live today is almost irresistibly biased toward an interpretation of these passages that condones a life more like that of decent people around us than like the life of Paul and his Lord. We talk about leading a different kind of life, but we also have ready explanations for not being really different. And with those explanations we have talked our way out of the very practices that alone would enable us to be citizens of another world."*[14]

Because these practices are so radical for us, it's wise to approach them in an experimental manor (not to mention that it's wise to approach them at all!). Something that is true of all spiritual practices, and particularly comes into play with silence and solitude, is that we need a long-term view. Our practice of silence and solitude is more about the way that they shape us over months, years, and decades of engaging in them rather than about a one-time experience. Just practicing them once leaves us wondering whether we got anything out of the experience or not. Remember—after all—this is about *waiting* on God and allowing him to work how he wants, when he wants, whether we even end up being aware of it or not.

So here are the simple, but very challenging, suggestions for waiting on God this Advent through silence and solitude:

- **Silence**: Waste five minutes per day with God, accomplishing absolutely nothing. You aren't studying the Bible, nor going through a prayer list, but just being quiet and seeking to increase your awareness that God is with you. You can go on a walk or drink a cup of coffee, but do something with your body that will remind the rest of you that you're spending this time with God. (In other words, doing laundry or paying bills won't help.) Your mind will become distracted, but don't let that concern you. That's more of a bother to you than it is to God.

- **Solitude**: *Option A* (Semi-Radical): Take advantage of the "little solitudes" that are already in your normal days. In other words, when you find yourself alone and able to choose what to do, don't waste the opportunity by turning on the TV immediately or checking Facebook one more time. Leave the radio off in the car while you're driving, or take whatever opportunities present themselves to enjoy being alone with God in the course of your normal days.

  *Option B (*More Radical): Take a full day sometime between now and Christmas to be alone with God. See Appendix B for some brief guidelines on how to do so.

A Prayer for the Day:

Almighty God, whose most dear Son went not up to joy but first he suffered pain, and entered not into glory before he was crucified: Mercifully grant that we, walking in the way of the cross, may find it none other than the way of life and peace; through Jesus Christ our Lord. Amen.

A Prayer for the Week:

Almighty God, give us grace to cast away the works of darkness, and put on the armor of light, now in the time of this mortal life in which your Son Jesus Christ came to visit us in great humility; that in the last day, when he shall come again in his glorious majesty to judge both the living and the dead, we may rise to the life immortal; through him who lives and reigns with you and the Holy Spirit, one God, now and for ever. Amen.

Wait—Learn to Love

WHENEVER WE GET TO SPEND THE HOLIDAYS with my wife's family, I always look forward to their tradition of watching what is perhaps the funniest Christmas movie ever made, *National Lampoon's Christmas Vacation*. Part of the reason the movie is so funny is that we can identify with both the Griswold family's eagerness to have relatives come to their house for Christmas, and their eagerness for it to be over as soon as possible. At one point, after the extended family begins to arrive at their house, Clark says to his wife, "Well, I'm going to park the cars, and get—check the luggage, and well, I'll be outside for—the season."

The "we're glad to see them come, and we're glad to see them go" sentiment is easy to identify with. [Just to clarify for any of my own relatives reading this: of course I'm speaking hypothetically. I hear that most other families are like this, but obviously I'm really looking forward to being with all of you—just like always. It's just unfortunate that while we're together, I'll occasionally have to be somewhere else to work on finding something new to write, or cars to park, or luggage to check....]

But here's the thing that holidays with our families can teach us: regardless of how alike or dislike your family may be to the Griswolds, you aren't going to go shopping for other families to spend Christmas with this year. Just because you may have your own living version of the movie's Cousin Eddie (or just because you may *be* the living version of Cousin

Eddie) doesn't make it likely that you're going to try to find a new family who is more fun to be with. We understand that our families are our families forever—even with all of their imperfections [again, dearest relatives, hypothetically here], they are the people who have been given to us to love.

A friend whom I admire greatly recently told me about a habit he has developed with people who cause him difficulty in life—whether they are family or not. On the surface, this will seem obvious and like it isn't anything profound, but its effects run deep. He said that, whenever there is someone who irritates him or causes him strain, he intentionally begins to pray daily for that person. He said, "You cannot help but to look at someone differently once you have been praying for them."

I am convinced that we need such simple and reliable advice in our relationships at many levels. We certainly need it in our family gatherings at this time of year. I mean—um—*you* probably need it in *your* family gatherings at this time of year. Yet there are other contexts where it is just as needed. I think that God has given us two primary circles of people who should provide the context in which we learn to love others and be loved by them: family and church.

So if you are one for whom family get-togethers during the holidays don't involve being around people with whom you would need to follow my friend's advice, surely your church can provide someone for you. If all of your family relationships are easy, go to church and you'll be sure to encounter someone more difficult! [Once again, dear church family—hypothetical!]

Yet how differently do we treat those two sets of relationships? Our families may annoy us, but we still get together with them year after year. However, if someone in church gets under our skin, we're likely to either seek to put them in their place or avoid them. If it's someone in our Sunday School class, we can stop attending or go find another.

Or, of course, we always carry the threat in our pockets of going to find another church.

When we do so, we completely miss the point: we are in these relationships to learn to love.

So my final suggestion in laying the groundwork this week for waiting on God throughout Advent is:

- Focus on learning to love those with whom God has already connected you—whether through family, church, or other relationships. Love them as they are without attempting to fix them or let them in on the great plan you have for their lives.

- Take my friend's advice in regard to any of your difficult relationships by praying for that person often—before, during, and after interacting with them. (Of course, now many of us may have a whole new reaction when someone at church mentions that they're praying for us!)

The connection between learning to love and our theme this week of practices for waiting on God may not seem as obvious as some of the previous days' suggestions, but we make a costly mistake if we ever separate our personal spiritual practices from our relationships. If I pray, read the Scriptures, take Communion, and spend ample time in silence and solitude, but am a selfish grouch, it's safe to say that I have not waited upon God in those practices but have only done them in ways that have allowed me to remain in control. Or from a positive angle, when we wait on God through these practices, as well as learn to love people through our ordinary relationships, we will find that the time we spend alone with God always, inevitably, has an effect on our relationships.

So far in our reflections, I have laid a foundation by digging into things that we can be doing to wait on God throughout Advent. For the rest of these weeks, we will begin exploring the stories that have shaped Advent for so many Christians for so long. While this week has focused on the present aspects of Advent (how Christ comes to dwell more fully in us now), tomorrow we turn a corner and look to the future. We now have some tools that will help us to heed the Bible's call to always be ready, but what is it that we're supposed to be ready for?

A Prayer for the Day:

Almighty God, who after the creation of the world rested from all your works and sanctified a day of rest for all your creatures: Grant that we, putting away all earthly anxieties, may be duly prepared for the service of your sanctuary, and that our rest here upon earth may be a preparation for the eternal rest promised to your people in heaven; through Jesus Christ our Lord. Amen.

A Prayer for the Week:

Almighty God, give us grace to cast away the works of darkness, and put on the armor of light, now in the time of this mortal life in which your Son Jesus Christ came to visit us in great humility; that in the last day, when he shall come again in his glorious majesty to judge both the living and the dead, we may rise to the life immortal; through him who lives and reigns with you and the Holy Spirit, one God, now and for ever. Amen.

Advent Future

A S A COLLEGE STUDENT, I took an elective course titled The New Testament and the End Times. I took it because, while others appeared as if they knew exactly what the Bible said about the future, I felt thoroughly confused about it. My sense of confusion about the Bible and the future began as a teenager when, during the Gulf War, I remember feeling intrigued and overwhelmed with how people in my church and the media were tying the political events of those days to prophecies in the Bible. I can remember the evening when President Bush announced Operation Desert Storm. I went to my room, opened my Bible, and came across some verse which convinced me the world was going to come to an end that night. As you might guess, it took me a while to fall asleep. I eventually did sleep though, and woke up the next morning with the world still in existence.

I was thankful to wake up the next day and realize that the world did not come to an end that night, but that didn't stop my confusion from increasing. Christian bookstores seemed to have an ever-increasing supply of books that deepened my sense of being on the outside of those who understood. It was like there was a code in the Bible that others had a secret key to unlock, but I hadn't yet figured any of it out.

So I took the elective course in college in the hope that it would help resolve my confusion. After being given the assignments of reading several books on the subject and studying the relevant passages in the Bible—I still felt thoroughly confused about what the Bible taught about the future. My consolation from that course was to come away convinced that things weren't spelled out in the Bible quite so directly as other people had seemed to think. The best memory I have of that semester is observing my professor, who knew the Bible thoroughly and had studied it diligently for decades, and seeing how he refused to speak to the issues with the "this is obviously what is going to happen" kind of confidence I had seen in Christian books and videos over the previous years. I didn't come out of the course with any answers, but—instead—enjoyed observing a New Testament scholar who had so many questions too.

I am attempting to make a point by describing all of this, but before I do, I'll acknowledge what may be going through some of your minds as you read this: "Why is he talking about the end of the world when these are supposed to be devotions about Christmas?" When we began last week, I described how Christian tradition teaches us that we will be better prepared for Christmas if we have the discipline to wait until it arrives, and it still isn't here yet. While the culture around us is into its Christmas season full-swing, many of Christ's people through the centuries have insisted that what we can best do during this time is to wait, because it's Advent.

Last week we considered how we can wait on God in our lives now, and this week we explore one of the main themes of Advent: we need to wait, always living ready and watchful for the day when Christ will return. Identifying that as our theme for the week may pique the interest of some of you, while for others it might create a knot in your stomach and make you want to skip this week's readings. If you'd rather read about, well—almost anything rather than what the Bible says about Christ's return, please hang in there with me. What I'm going to say about it is almost surely different, and better news, than what you've heard.

Regardless of where you fall on the spectrum of interest in the topic, Christ's return is simultaneously one of the most confusing and most popular topics among Christians today. How are we supposed to wait readily for it when it proves so difficult to understand anything about it?

I'm going to spend the rest of the week passing along guidance which I have found to be very helpful in considering what the Bible teaches about the future, but first I'll give you fair warning: some of what I'm going to say will likely meddle with your understanding of parts of Scripture. Before the week is over, we will cover ground that gives us very good news, but in order to get there, we will need to evaluate some of the things we already assume the Bible says.

In addition to the practices of waiting that we covered last week, to set this week's stage for the way that Advent trains us to wait on what God has in store for our future, I invite you to join me in praying as often as you think about it the simple prayer that is the exclamation point at the end of the book of Revelation:

Come, Lord Jesus!

A Prayer for the Day:

O God, you make us glad with the weekly remembrance of the glorious resurrection of your Son our Lord: Give us this day such blessing through our worship of you, that the week to come may be spent in your favor; through Jesus Christ our Lord. Amen.

A Prayer for the Week:

Merciful God, who sent your messengers the prophets to preach repentance and prepare the way for our salvation: Give us grace to heed their warnings and forsake our sins, that we may greet with joy the coming of Jesus Christ our Redeemer; who lives and reigns with you and the Holy Spirit, one God, now and for ever. Amen.

What We Aren't Waiting For

I WAS RECENTLY ENTERTAINED ONLINE by a reviewer of Christian books as I browsed their annual list of the year's worst Christian book covers. Their prize-winner for 2012 was the cover of a commentary on Revelation which depicted a gray-haired elderly man standing and pointing down a road toward a dark sky with his other arm around the shoulder of a boy, possibly his grandson. The subtitle of the book was "Hope Beyond the Horizon," which highlighted the object in the distance to which the grandfather was pointing the boy's attention: a mushroom cloud. The reviewer's comment, though sarcastic, identified the irony in thinking of any such event as being the Christian hope: "Look there, Sonny, it's our long-awaited hope, appearing just beyond the horizon...and it's a nuclear explosion!"[15]

Of course, frightening images of people's interpretations of biblical prophecies aren't hard to find. The *Left Behind* series of books was incredibly popular, and (I would argue) has had more effect on the beliefs about what the Bible teaches than has the Bible itself for many people in our culture. I certainly don't have a problem with authors and Bible teachers communicating their interpretations of Scripture in the most effective ways that they can. However, when interpretations of difficult passages of Scripture become so popularized, we can unknowingly begin to think we're familiar with what the Bible teaches, even if it turns out that we've only actually become familiar with an idea from a trendy book or movie. Then, we fail to ever wrestle with what the Bible actually says.

This week, I want to clarify what I understand to be the biblical picture of the events in the future for which Advent is our annual reminder to wait readily. In order to do so, in today's reflection I'll look at some views of the future which I think are inaccurate. Then, for the rest of the week, we'll do our best to consider what Jesus and the writers of Scripture were indeed trying to communicate.

From the previous paragraphs, you probably won't be surprised for me to state that I disagree with the widespread ideas about the end times which are communicated in many places by many people, most notably through the *Left Behind* series over the past couple of decades. For many of us, though, it may be a surprise that any other interpretations even exist.

I mentioned yesterday how I was a teenager during the years around the Gulf War, and I can remember the intensity with which connections were being made between biblical passages and the political events of those days. Because there were so many Christian books and videos identifying that period as possibly being the "end times," I assumed that even if they were wrong about the timing of the events they were predicting, I had no reason to doubt that the coming of those events was clearly prophesied in the Bible. In other words, because I so often heard Christians with more knowledge than me talking about things like the Great Tribulation, the Rapture, someone who would be identified as the Antichrist, and the end of the world in general, I assumed that the Bible taught those things.[16]

I accepted those interpretations because of my limited knowledge of the Scripture and because I was unaware of any alternatives. I can remember being shocked when a college friend who was a Bible major mentioned in conversation that he didn't believe there would be a rapture. I thought, "this guy is a Bible major and he doesn't even believe what the Bible says!" He challenged the beliefs that I had inherited from my culture, and as I have studied the Scriptures in the years since then, I am thankful that he did.

I don't think it would be particularly useful to spend much effort detailing why I think these others' interpretations are wrong. What I would rather do is to assure any of you for whom these widespread conceptions of the future don't sit well that they are not the only possible interpretations. In fact, they have only become popular since the beginning of the 20th century, and mostly in North America. Christians in other parts of the world today and for centuries have looked at the Bible in different ways.

What matters here is this: For what are we hoping? Advent is our annual reminder to live in a constant ready waiting, but for what?

To be honest, if the Bible insisted that our future includes a Great Tribulation, Rapture, Antichrist, and end of the world, I wouldn't want to wait for that. I certainly wouldn't long for it in hope—the only thing I would hope would be that I could somehow avoid all of it. Instead of these things which I'm proposing we *aren't* waiting for, we will clarify a longstanding Christian view of Jesus' return, judgment (and why it's a good thing), resurrection, and new creation. My hope is that with our lenses cleaned and better able to see ahead, we will be better able to join centuries of God's people in waiting for Christ's return and more clearly understand how to live and wait on God daily from now until then.

A Prayer for the Day:

O God, the King eternal, whose light divides the day from the night and turns the shadow of death into the morning: Drive far from us all wrong desires, incline our hearts to keep your law, and guide our feet into the way of peace; that, having done your will with cheerfulness while it was day, we may, when night comes, rejoice to give you thanks; through Jesus Christ our Lord. Amen.

A Prayer for the Week:

Merciful God, who sent your messengers the prophets to preach repentance and prepare the way for our salvation: Give us grace to heed their warnings and forsake our sins, that we may greet with joy the coming of Jesus Christ our Redeemer; who lives and reigns with you and the Holy Spirit, one God, now and for ever. Amen.

What We Are Waiting For

IF THE POPULAR UNDERSTANDING OF THE END TIMES that we discussed yesterday is indeed not what we're waiting for, and there are other legitimate interpretations of the relevant passages of Scripture, then what are they? What is it that we are waiting for throughout Advent each year—and throughout our entire lives as followers of Jesus? At this point in writing this series of reflections, I'm now realizing that I have a serious challenge on my hands (a little late to be realizing this). The fact that there are such widely varying interpretations of these passages of Scripture should let us know that the writers of the Bible were trying to communicate things that were difficult for them to express. They were highly competent writers, who took part in writing the most widely-read and most influential book in world history. Apparently when I was planning this book, I had the faulty thought that I might be able to clarify in a few days' devotions what it was difficult for them to find the language to say. I think taking up this challenge is worth a shot, though, because it will be a tough job for any of us to practice Advent's waiting unless we have a better idea of what it is that we're waiting for. Therefore, I'll attempt to be both brief and say quite a bit to summarize this today, and then we'll spend the next three days unpacking it.

One of my favorite hymns is "This is My Father's World," and it has a couple of lines that grip me every time we sing them:

This is my Father's world. O let me ne'er forget
That though the wrong seems oft so strong, God is the ruler yet.
This is my Father's world: the battle is not done:
Jesus Who died shall be satisfied, and earth and heav'n be one.[17]

The idea of earth and heaven being united, with the vindicated, crucified and risen Jesus in the center as King, is surprisingly foreign to the way that I had previously thought about Jesus' return, yet I have become convinced that it is indicated as God's original intent and mission throughout history from the beginning of the Bible until its dramatic "Come, Lord Jesus!" conclusion at the end of Revelation.[18]

While I previously thought we were looking toward a dreadful end of the world, the Bible speaks instead of "the end of the age" and "the age to come." Instead of thinking that the world will be destroyed as we escape it, the scriptural hope is that the world will be made new.

I previously mentioned how helpful N.T. Wright's *For Everyone* commentaries on the New Testament have been to me, and one of the things about them that either points to how incredibly beneficial they are, or to just how nerdy I am, is that they're the first books in which I've ever paid close attention not just to the text itself, but also to the glossary. Any of us could increase our level of biblical literacy dramatically just by studying his glossary, because Wright clears up the meanings of so many biblical terms which usually—at best—only carry vague meanings in our minds, even though we hear and use them often.

The glossary's paragraph on "Second Coming" is worth a long quotation here, as it gives us a framework for the rest of this week's explorations. There's plenty packed into these words to chew on for a while, so you may want to read it more than once:

When God renews the whole creation, as he has promised, bringing together heaven and earth, Jesus himself will be at the centre of it all, personally present to and with his people and ruling his world fully and finally at last. The Christian hope picks up, and gives more explicit focus to, the ancient Jewish hope that [Yahweh] would in the end return to his people to judge and to save. Since the ascension is often thought of in terms of Jesus' "going away", this final moment is often thought of in terms of his "coming back again", hence the shorthand "second coming". However, since the ascension in fact means that Jesus, though now invisible, is not far away but rather closely present with us, it isn't surprising that some of the key New Testament passages speak not of his "return" as though from a great distance, but of his "appearing" (e.g. Colossians 3:4; 1 John 3:2). The early Christians expected this "appearing" to take place not necessarily within a generation as is often thought (because of a misreading of Mark 13 and similar passages), but at any time—which could be immediate or delayed. This caused a problem for some early Christians (2 Peter 3:3-10), but not for many. For the early Christians, the really important event—the resurrection of Jesus—had already taken place, and his final "appearing" would simply complete what had then been decisively begun.[19]

In contrast to the Great Tribulation/Rapture/Antichrist view of the end of the world we described yesterday, I want to wait for Jesus to come again, finally and fully reigning as King, setting everything right and making everything new as Wright describes above. That kind of hope stirs my longing to see it come to pass rather than my desire to be part of history that won't have to witness it.

Most importantly for our discussions here, I can order my Advent—and indeed, my life—around waiting for the day when we will see Jesus as I seek to live always ready for it, constantly preparing my soul and the area of the world over which I have any say to be ready and able to welcome Jesus as King.

Over the next three days, we'll look more closely at three aspects of Jesus' return, and how they shape our Advent hope:

judgment (and why it's a good thing), resurrection, and new creation. Then, we'll finish the week by considering how we can live now in light of what's to come.

A Prayer for the Day:

O God, the author of peace and lover of concord, to know you is eternal life and to serve you is perfect freedom: Defend us, your humble servants, in all assaults of our enemies; that we, surely trusting in your defense, may not fear the power of any adversaries; through the might of Jesus Christ our Lord. Amen.

A Prayer for the Week:

Merciful God, who sent your messengers the prophets to preach repentance and prepare the way for our salvation: Give us grace to heed their warnings and forsake our sins, that we may greet with joy the coming of Jesus Christ our Redeemer; who lives and reigns with you and the Holy Spirit, one God, now and for ever. Amen.

Why We Long for Jesus' Appearing: Judgment (and Why It's a Good Thing)

*Beloved, while you are **waiting** for these things, strive to be found by him at peace, without spot or blemish.*
(2 Peter 3:14)

WE BEGAN THESE ADVENT REFLECTIONS last week as I wondered what it would be like to come to Christmas this year with a soul well-prepared to celebrate Jesus' birth, and I tried to point out how Christian tradition provides a different, seemingly indirect way of preparing by waiting through Advent. Though Advent's themes will come closer to Bethlehem as its days wind down, until those final days before Christmas, we are encouraged to consider themes quite different from those that normally come to mind with images of the nativity. If we follow the culture's calendar and consider ourselves to already be in the Christmas season rather than waiting for it, we probably won't give much thought during this time to the importance of topics like waiting, longing, Christ's return, resurrection, or new creation. If we have already mentally put the baby in the manger, we're certainly also unlikely to ponder today's topic, which the Advent Scriptures point us toward repeatedly: judgment.

On the other hand, if we practice the patience of waiting through Advent and listen attentively to the Scriptures through these weeks, the topic of judgment won't be far from our minds. We are warned to be on guard so that our hearts aren't weighed down with immorality or the worries of this life. We are reminded to live our lives as if we are workers caring for our master's things while he is away, always being mindful that he could return at any moment. If we notice any ways that our lives have become out of line, we're urged to heed John the Baptist's call to repent and prepare the way for our King's return, so that when he comes our lives would be like trees producing the kind of fruit expected of them.

Be ready. Keep awake. Stay alert. Live honorably. Salvation is near. Be blameless.

Yet I suspect that if most of us were to write the things we longingly wait for in life, God's judgment would appear on very few lists. One reason for that could be that we are legitimately unprepared for it, like the student who dreads taking a spelling test because they chose to watch a movie instead of study their words. If that's the case, you can do something about it, which is why we began last week by discussing practical ways that we can wait on God now.

For most of us, however, our lack of longing for God's judgment comes from a misunderstanding of it. With the subject being our lives rather than spelling words, we may all feel like that unprepared student, and the stakes here are higher than a grade on a spelling quiz. Since the Scriptures insist that we will be judged and should therefore live readily for it, it matters immensely how we think about the one who will be judging us.

Here again, I think we've been overly influenced by popular images of the end times. They present us with a Clint Eastwood-esque picture of God's judgment: He's the sheriff who's been away for some time before riding back into town with infinitely loaded pistols firing from each hand, annihilating anyone who's caused any trouble in his absence (and scaring the wits out of anyone else who he sees fit to leave standing). It's pretty difficult to reconcile that image of God with the loving Father of Jesus, and—like the grandfather pointing to a mushroom cloud discussed on Monday—it's hard to sincerely think of that as the hope for which we wait during Advent.

Among the many biblical metaphors for our relationship with God, one of the most common is that of a loving Father with his children, and I think we can better understand God's judgment in that context. *God is a loving parent who is resolutely working against the things that destroy his beloved children, and when Christ returns, that work—already achieved in Jesus' life, death, and resurrection—will be brought to final and full completion.*

The Scripture's insistence that there will be a judgment assures us that God is not like the never-judging overindulgent parent, described well by James Bryan Smith:

> *This god is like permissive parents who let their kids drink and do drugs and have sex without guilt. When we were young, we thought they were cool, but they weren't; they were lazy and did not really love their kids....These may be the kinds of parents you think you want when you are fifteen, but you really don't.*
>
> *I don't want a god who says, "It's cool. Don't sweat it...." This god does not love me. Being soft on sin is not loving, because sin destroys. I want a God who hates anything that hurts me. Hate is a strong word, but a good one. Because the true God not only hates what destroys me (sin and alienation) but also has taken steps to destroy my destroyer, I love him.*[20]

When Christ returns, as the Apostles' Creed states, "he will come to judge the living and the dead." This is great news, because it means that the victory over sin that he won on the cross—by taking the judgment against sin upon himself—will be completed. Everything that destroys us will finally and fully be dealt with—both the kinds of things that are outside of us which we lament in the news each day, and the ones that run right through our own hearts—everything will be made right when he comes as judge.

Of course part of that judgment will mean that those who refuse to allow God to be God will be granted their wish and finally be able to live free of him, with the kinds of consequences that we would expect whenever a proud child refuses the guidance of a knowledgeable and loving parent. As C.S. Lewis has described so masterfully in *The Great Divorce*, no one is dragged to heaven or hell kicking and screaming. Rather, God will simply allow us to have that which we have chosen.

Along with God's people through the centuries, I have chosen to be his. There are parts of my world, and parts of me, that need to be set right. Therefore, trusting God as my loving Father, and knowing myself to be his beloved child, I eagerly await that day "when he shall come again in power and great triumph to judge the world, [when we will] without shame or fear rejoice to behold his appearing."[21]

Judgment is how God will finally deal with the sin that destroys us. Tomorrow we turn our attention to what will happen because God has dealt with our other great destroyer, death: we will be resurrected.

A Prayer for the Day:

Lord God, almighty and everlasting Father, you have brought us in safety to this new day: Preserve us with your mighty power, that we may not fall into sin, nor be overcome by adversity; and in all we do, direct us to the fulfilling of your purpose; through Jesus Christ our Lord. Amen.

A Prayer for the Week:

Merciful God, who sent your messengers the prophets to preach repentance and prepare the way for our salvation: Give us grace to heed their warnings and forsake our sins, that we may greet with joy the coming of Jesus Christ our Redeemer; who lives and reigns with you and the Holy Spirit, one God, now and for ever. Amen.

Why We Long for Jesus' Appearing: Resurrection

ONCE ATTENDED SOMETHING MY FELLOW METHODISTS and I call "License to Preach School," and as you might guess by its title, part of what we learned there was guidance for preaching sermons. Each participant was required to write a sermon during the days of the course and then preach it to a small group of peers for feedback.

I was excited about my opportunity. I worked on a sermon, and I thought that it was pretty good. In my mind, I was imagining the kind of congratulatory feedback that my classmates and supervisors were going to give me. My turn came, I preached my sermon, and I felt like things were going well. When the time for feedback came, people were a little hesitant. (I thought, "Well, of course. I've just given them a lot to think about. It's probably a challenge for them to express in words how much my sermon has impacted them." Remember—this was License to Preach School, not a License of Humility.) Then, finally, someone spoke up and just as I expected—they started to talk about how much they enjoyed my sermon and what they got out of it. Two or three others followed suit, saying that those same parts of the sermon were helpful as well.

There were two problems that quickly caught my attention about their comments: first, the parts of the sermon they described as helpful weren't in any way intended to be part of my point. Second, though I imagined myself to have driven my main point home with great effectiveness, no one ever mentioned anything close to what I wanted to communicate. The thing I intended to emphasize was apparently completely missed, while they picked up on other things that I hadn't even really wanted to say.

Something of the same dynamic happens in many of our discussions about Jesus' return, but for a different reason. In the case of my preaching, my classmates' feedback was evidence that I had not been as effective of a communicator as I had fancied myself to be, and therefore my point was missed. The same thing happens with the Bible, though in the case of the Scriptures, the fault isn't on the communicators' side, but on ours as the audience. We often read and see the things that we want to see in the Bible regardless of what is actually there, plus many inherent factors come into play in trying to correctly interpret a complex ancient document from a culture very different from our own. Yet the result is still the same: we miss the main points. In the case of what the Bible says about our future and the things that will happen when Jesus returns, our normal conversations tend to focus on all kinds of side-issues, while leaving out the Scripture's main emphasis when it speaks of the age to come: *resurrection*.

When Christ returns—on that day when all of these centuries of longing and waiting for him finally end, when this yearning ache we have for him to appear is finally satisfied and there is no more need for this painful yet hopeful waiting of Advent—the two great destroyers of his people will be utterly and definitively dealt with: sin and death. Sin's defeat was achieved in Jesus' death on the cross, and—as we discussed yesterday—its downfall will be full and final when Jesus returns for judgment. Death's defeat was achieved in

Jesus' resurrection on Easter Sunday, and its vanquishment will come when what happened to Jesus happens to all of us, and we are raised to indestructible life in new, death-defeating bodies like that of our Lord.

When the Scriptures say that death has lost its sting and been swallowed up in victory, it isn't just spouting optimistic nonsense. Because of Jesus—the one who could defeat death, because he was the one who could defeat sin, because of the eternal kind of life that was in him through his knowledge of his loving Father—*life* will have the last word from that day on. Suffering will cease and be redeemed. Those whom we have loved and lost will be seen again. Everyone who has laid down their life for his sake will rise and find it.

If in our lives as followers of Jesus, the only time that we think about and talk of resurrection is on Easter Sunday, we have missed the point. Exceedingly. On the other hand, if we live in hopeful waiting expectation of the day when our King returns, sets everything right, and we will all be made alive in him forever, then Advent will have taken its intended effect upon us.

Then, one day, he will come, and we will be ready.

A Prayer for the Day:

Heavenly Father, in you we live and move and have our being: We humbly pray you so to guide and govern us by your Holy Spirit, that in all the cares and occupations of our life we may not forget you, but may remember that we are ever walking in your sight; through Jesus Christ our Lord. Amen.

A Prayer for the Week:

Merciful God, who sent your messengers the prophets to preach repentance and prepare the way for our salvation: Give us grace to heed their warnings and forsake our sins, that we may greet with joy the coming of Jesus Christ our Redeemer; who lives and reigns with you and the Holy Spirit, one God, now and for ever. Amen.

Second Friday of Advent

Why We Long for Jesus' Appearing: New Creation

*I consider that the sufferings of this present time are not worth comparing with the glory about to be revealed to us. For the creation **waits** with eager longing for the revealing of the children of God; for the creation was subjected to futility, not of its own will but by the will of the one who subjected it, in hope that the creation itself will be set free from its bondage to decay and will obtain the freedom of the glory of the children of God. We know that the whole creation has been groaning in labor pains until now; and not only the creation, but we ourselves, who have the first fruits of the Spirit, groan inwardly while we **wait** for adoption, the redemption of our bodies. For in hope we were saved. Now hope that is seen is not hope. For who hopes for what is seen? But if we hope for what we do not see, we **wait** for it with patience.*
(Romans 8:18-25)

WHAT WERE YOU AND I MADE TO DO? If someone has been engaged in work that is a good fit for them, we often speak of them as having been born to do that particular thing. I have a friend whom I can say with confidence was born to be a teacher. I've known people who were apparently born to be farmers, or to work with animals, or to be engineers. My own vocation isn't quite so clear—particularly during this time of year, I feel like I may have been born to eat Christmas cookies. Even though I'm closer to the end of the spectrum of the people in mid-life or later who are still wondering what they want to be when they grow up, I'm still grateful to—occasionally—have had moments when something I have worked on has brought a great sense of fulfillment, a feeling of having done the kind of thing I was created to do rather than just wasting my days.

Regardless of how clearly each of us can think about the question of what we were made to do, here it is from a different angle: What were you and I made to do—forever? If we have bought into inaccurate understandings of what the Bible says about our future, our thoughts about the nature of our existence forever will surely also be skewed, and—honestly—we've been given some pretty silly images for what we might actually be doing "when we've been there ten thousand years" and beyond. Sometimes we're told that heaven will be similar to an unending worship service. I've had people make comments to me indicating their belief that we will grow wings and fly around among the clouds. I'm sure you can probably think of other forms of these ideas, and I'm convinced (and relieved) that they are not the biblical picture of eternity.

We can zero in on some of the dissimilarities between popular thinking about our life in heaven and what the Bible says about our future by looking again at that line from the last stanza of Amazing Grace I quoted above, "when we've been there ten thousand years..." Where is the *there* we expect to be for so long?

Even though we often think that our eternity with God will be spent in a vague amorphous "up there," from the beginning of the Bible in Genesis to its conclusion at the end of Revelation, part of the understanding of what it means to be human is that we are meant to exist and glorify God *forever, right here, within creation*. In other words, our expectation as Christians isn't that we'll be going away to some never-ending non-bodily existence, but that when Christ returns, we will experience resurrection as he did and the veil now separating heaven and earth will be removed "and earth and heav'n be one."

Part of what this means is that just as we have work to do now, we will have work to do then. What we will do forever in this new creation will be similar to what Genesis says humans were given the task of doing in the original creation: to have dominion over it, care for it and cultivate it. The number of ways we could possibly do this is surely limitless, and as Paul described in the passage quoted above, creation itself is eagerly awaiting us to take our proper place and participate fully in the work of God's kingdom *in creation—forever*.

Two of the writers who have influenced me most deeply have both written about this, and their words are worth quoting directly. First, from Dallas Willard, one of the most hopeful, challenging, and meaning-packed few sentences I've ever read:

> *We should not think of ourselves as destined to be celestial bureaucrats, involved eternally in celestial "administrivia." That would be only slightly better than being caught in an everlasting church service. No, we should think of our destiny as being absorbed in a tremendously creative team effort, with unimaginably splendid leadership, on an inconceivably vast plane of activity, with ever more comprehensive cycles of productivity and enjoyment.*[22]

That alone should give each of us enough to think about for, well, ten thousand years or so. And N.T. Wright summarizes much of what I have attempted to say throughout this week:

> *The New Testament picks up from the Old the theme that God intends, in the end, to put the whole creation to rights. Earth and heaven were made to overlap with one another, not fitfully, mysteriously, and partially as they do at the moment, but completely, gloriously, and utterly. "The earth shall be filled with the glory of God as the waters cover the sea." That is the*

promise which resonates throughout the Bible story, from Isaiah (and behind him, by implication, from Genesis itself) all the way through to Paul's greatest visionary moments and the final chapters of the book of Revelation. The great drama will end, not with "saved souls" being snatched up into heaven, away from the wicked earth and the mortal bodies which have dragged them down into sin, but with the New Jerusalem coming down from heaven to earth, so that "the dwelling of God is with humans" (Revelation 21:3).

...God's plan is not to abandon this world, the world which he said was "very good." Rather, he intends to remake it. And when he does, he will raise all his people to new bodily life to live in it. That is the promise of the Christian gospel. To live in it, yes; and also to rule over it. There is a mystery here which few today have even begun to ponder. Both Paul and Revelation stress that in God's new world those who belong to the Messiah will be placed in charge. The first creation was put into the care of God's image-bearing creatures. The new creation will be put into the wise, healing stewardship of those who have been "renewed according to the image of the creator," as Paul puts it (Colossians 3:10).[23]

We have attempted to cover a lot of ground very quickly this week, and tomorrow we'll consider what it all means for us now. If this is the picture the Bible gives us of what's to come and is that for which we are waiting during Advent, how should we live now because of it?

A Prayer for the Day:

Almighty God, whose most dear Son went not up to joy but first he suffered pain, and entered not into glory before he was crucified: Mercifully grant that we, walking in the way of the cross, may find it none other than the way of life and peace; through Jesus Christ our Lord. Amen.

A Prayer for the Week:

Merciful God, who sent your messengers the prophets to preach repentance and prepare the way for our salvation: Give us grace to heed their warnings and forsake our sins, that we may greet with joy the coming of Jesus Christ our Redeemer; who lives and reigns with you and the Holy Spirit, one God, now and for ever. Amen.

How to Live Now in Light of What's to Come

I'VE ATTEMPTED TO SAY SOME THINGS this week that may have ruffled some people's feathers. Don't feel bad if your brain is tired from reading it—if that's the case, I'm glad you've stuck with me to this point. Even though I wrote it, I just re-read it, and I got tired. It's been a mental stretch, and for some of us a challenge to some long-held beliefs, but I want to wrap up this week's focus on the future aspects of Advent by reminding us of why it all matters.

1 Corinthians 15 is a tremendously important passage for us as Christians. There, Paul goes to great lengths to remind the Corinthians about the centrality of the resurrection for them. He reminds them of the account of Jesus' resurrection, his appearances to disciples before his ascension and why it matters immensely that he was resurrected in a real physical body. He talks about that day when Christ will return and all of his people will be resurrected in imperishable bodies like Christ's (or transformed into them if they are still living on that day) when death is finally defeated for all of God's people.

Then, immediately after the climax of the passage where Paul emphasizes how "death is swallowed up in victory," he closes his long argument about the centrality of the resurrection for all Christians with a statement that might surprise us:

"Therefore, my beloved, be steadfast, immovable, always excelling in the work of the Lord, because you know that in the Lord your labor is not in vain."[24]

Although we wouldn't say it this way, we tend to think the opposite: if Christ is coming again and everything will be set straight, with the world and even our own bodies being made new, we often think whatever happens between now and then is beside the point. Sure we intend to do well, but any efforts at discipleship and service are viewed as extras which will be nice if we get to them, but if not—as long as we're on Jesus' side at the end of all of it—we're okay.

That attitude can't exist within Paul's thinking. His point in urging us to be steadfast—precisely because of what he's said about Christ's return and how our own resurrection will happen as Jesus' did—is that our lives now are of interminable importance. Because we will be given new bodies on that day, what we do in our bodies now is a way of becoming either more or less prepared for the kind of lives with God that we will lead forever. And because we are made to extend God's reign in creation rather than to escape creation, how we relate to creation now is practice for the responsibilities that will be entrusted to us according to the character that we have allowed God to develop in us.

Again, N.T. Wright's words are instructive:

The truth of the resurrection of the dead and the transformation of the living is not just a truth about the future hope. It's a truth about the present significance of what we are and do. If it is true that God is going to transform this present world, and renew our whole selves, bodies included, then what we do in the present time with our bodies, and with our world, matters.[25]

Every time we show kindness, it matters. Every time we manage something well, it matters. Every time we make a decision to do the right thing when no one is looking, it matters. Every time we choose to arrange our lives in ways that give God more space to abide in us, it matters. These things have effects now that will still be resonating on the day when our King returns. As he himself said, "just as you do it to one of the least of these who are members of my family, you did it to me."

When we look at it in this way, we realize that our waiting doesn't only happen during Advent, but that every day of our lives as Christians is spent waiting for Christ's return. We open our lives to him in the ways we discussed last week (through prayer, reading the Scriptures, Holy Communion, solitude, silence, and loving service to others) as a way of waiting on his return. When he comes, we want to be found to be like him, already at home in the kind of world over which he will reign forever. So, we begin practicing the eternal kind of life now, and until we see him, we continue to pray again that great Advent prayer with which we began this week:

Come, Lord Jesus!

A Prayer for the Day:

Almighty God, who after the creation of the world rested from all your works and sanctified a day of rest for all your creatures: Grant that we, putting away all earthly anxieties, may be duly prepared for the service of your sanctuary, and that our rest here upon earth may be a preparation for the eternal rest promised to your people in heaven; through Jesus Christ our Lord. Amen.

A Prayer for the Week:

Merciful God, who sent your messengers the prophets to preach repentance and prepare the way for our salvation: Give us grace to heed their warnings and forsake our sins, that we may greet with joy the coming of Jesus Christ our Redeemer; who lives and reigns with you and the Holy Spirit, one God, now and for ever. Amen.

The Story Jesus Lived In

THERE'S A DIFFERENCE BETWEEN OUR ACQUAINTANCES and those we really know well, and much of that difference comes down to how well we know the story of their life.

You may have a coworker with whom you interact on a daily basis. They may be pleasant to work with, and you may even consider yourselves friends. However, with most of our coworkers, we don't really know the stories they live in—we don't know what their childhood was like or where their grandparents were from. We may not know if they have siblings, if they've always dealt with addictions, or whether they grew up in the city or in the country. They probably don't know those kinds of things about you either, and that's okay because of the kind of relationship you have as coworkers.

To contrast the difference it makes when we know someone's story, think of another kind of relationship: someone with whom you were close friends as a child, but now have contact with no more often than a couple of times per year. Your interactions with an old friend happen much less often than they do with your coworker, but yet there's a sense in which you still know them significantly because you know their story. You have memories of spending time in their house with their families. You can remember some painful experience they had as well as a time when they were happy. You know whether their story began in poverty or riches. You might even be able to explain some of the course that their life has taken because you know their story so well.

To really know someone well, you would have both sides of the relationships described above: the knowledge of their story plus the continued daily interactions, but I've realized that isn't how we normally think of knowing Jesus. We tend to focus on knowing Jesus in the ways that we would know a coworker. Sure, there are some obvious differences between what it would be like to know the Son of God through daily interactions and what it's like to know the person in the office next to you, but here's my point: if we don't really know another person without knowing the story they live in, neither do we really know Jesus without knowing the story he lived in. *Jesus' story is the long and winding story of ancient Israel, and if we don't know that story, we don't have a chance at understanding who he was nor of comprehending many of the things he said and did.* Advent is always a reminder of that story.

I recently installed a new game on my phone for my kids to play. It was a Bible app, with narration of different biblical stories and games, puzzles, etc. that the kids enjoy playing. Something caught my attention about it, though, when I looked at it for the first time and noticed the Bible stories that it includes. The first story was about God creating heaven and earth. The second story was about Adam and Eve's sin in the Garden of Eden, and then the next story was...Christmas. There was no Abraham, Moses, David, nor Elijah, even though the New Testament constantly refers to them in its attempts to understand and communicate who Jesus was and what he did.

Unfortunately, though, that children's Bible app is characteristic of the way we often think about Jesus. If our theology ultimately skips straight from Eden to Bethlehem, we have an utterly context-less Jesus, and we are bound to either misinterpret or be left scratching our heads at the majority of the New Testament's content.

We began this Advent adventure two weeks ago by focusing on practical methods of waiting on God now, through daily interaction with him in our present lives. Last week, we looked to the future and sought to clarify how we are part of two millennia of followers of Jesus who have waited on his return. This week, we look to the past, seeking to understand the story Jesus lived in by remembering ancient Israel's long waiting for the Messiah to come.

A Prayer for the Day:

O God, you make us glad with the weekly remembrance of the glorious resurrection of your Son our Lord: Give us this day such blessing through our worship of you, that the week to come may be spent in your favor; through Jesus Christ our Lord. Amen.

A Prayer for the Week:

Stir up your power, O Lord, and with great might come among us; and, because we are sorely hindered by our sins, let your bountiful grace and mercy speedily help and deliver us; through Jesus Christ our Lord, to whom, with you and the Holy Spirit, be honor and glory, now and for ever. Amen.

Israel's Longing for the King

I F WE WANT TO GET TO KNOW THE STORY JESUS LIVED IN, one of the most helpful places we can start is also one of the most unlikely. If you open your Bible to the first page of the New Testament, you will see Matthew's genealogy of Jesus. Most of us pay about as much attention to that opening passage of Matthew as we do to acknowledgements listed in the preface when we open a new book, and there are some similarities: in both cases, there is a list of people's names—most of whom we don't know, and the author is indicating that the book wouldn't have come into being without them. Nonetheless, we assume that the people named have no real significance for understanding the content of the book. While that may be the case with most things we read, it isn't what Matthew intended nor what his earliest readers would have thought when they read that list of names. If we dig into it a little bit, we can see that Matthew's list is less like an inconsequential roll of names who preceded Jesus by historical accident, and more like a way of beginning the book with a drum roll, trumpets blowing, and a royal herald calling for everyone's attention. [26] One way that Matthew makes this clear is by dividing his list into three sections:

In the first section, the first three names are Abraham, Isaac, and Jacob, which immediately lets us know that the story Matthew is about to tell us is *a thoroughly Jewish story*. In contrast to the understanding of the gospel represented in the children's Bible app I described yesterday, Matthew can't tell his version of the story by saying, "Once there were a man and woman who lived in the Garden of Eden who sinned....[and then skip to Matthew 1:18] Now the birth of Jesus took place this way...." No, for readers of the gospel, Jesus' story is always a story of the descendants of Abraham, Isaac, and Jacob. Matthew's beginning indicates that if we don't understand the Jewish story, we won't understand Jesus.

The second section of the list indicates that not only is Matthew about to tell us a Jewish story, but it will be *a story about Jewish royalty*. Not only is it going to be a story of a descendant of Abraham, Isaac, and Jacob, but also of one who traced his lineage through the royal line of David and Solomon. Almost all Jews of Jesus' day would have pointed to Abraham as their ancestor, but only a select few could claim to be a part of the line of David, Solomon, and the kings of Judah. It won't take long in this story to encounter Herod, who though he had the title, "King of the Jews," had no royal blood, and Matthew has already made it clear who has the right to the throne.

If that wasn't enough to pique our interest, the third section of the genealogy identifies the story as *a messianic story*. The third section begins with names of people who lived at the time when the kingdom of Judah was conquered, the center of their national identity (the Temple) was destroyed, and many of the descendants of Abraham were carried off from the land God had promised them into exile in Babylon. The prophets during the exile indicated that God would restore David's royal line and keep the promise that one of his descendants would be on the throne forever. Even though Jesus' ancestors had geographically returned from exile, they had never fully regained their freedom and therefore had a sense that the exile wasn't really over. They needed a deliverer who would free them from the oppression of their enemies. Even though Herod was rebuilding the Temple, there was no way he could fit the bill of their deliverer. They needed the one anointed

(*Messiah* in Hebrew, or *Christ* in Greek) by God to rescue them and fulfill God's promises.

In Matthew's telling, each of these three sections of the genealogy included fourteen generations, which is also packed full of meaning. Particularly in Jewish symbolism, the number seven was a symbol of completion. Jesus was born, not at a random point in history nor in a chance place in this genealogy, but as the first one in the seventh seven of generations. As N.T. Wright comments, "Jesus isn't just one member in an ongoing family, but actually the goal of the whole list....This birth, Matthew is saying, is what Israel has been waiting for for two thousand years."[27]

Having (in week one) considered some of the present aspects of Advent through the practices we can put in place in our lives which train us to wait on God's abiding in us now, and then (last week) explored the future aspects of Advent as we wait for Christ's return, this week, we look to strengthen our Advent waiting by looking in our rearview mirror and remembering ancient Israel's Advent longing as they waited for the Messiah to come. To be able to do so, we have to begin by clarifying what the term *Messiah* means to us and what it meant to ancient Israel as they waited through centuries for his coming.

When we read, for example, Peter's confession, "You are the Messiah, the Son of the living God," we read into that from our perspective now, thinking that Peter understood Jesus to be God. Rather, both the titles *Messiah (Christ)* and *son of God* were ways of Peter saying the same thing Matthew has said in his genealogy: Jesus was the promised, long-awaited, rightful king who had come at last to deliver Israel from her enemies.[28]

Matthew's genealogy sets up the story in one more vital way, by warning the reader that God accomplishes his purposes in unforeseen, even seemingly bizarre, ways. Matthew goes out of his way to include three names in Jesus' messianic, royal, Jewish lineage: Tamar (who tricked her father-in-law into sleeping with her by pretending to be a prostitute), Rahab (a prostitute in Jericho), and "the wife of Uriah the Hittite," whom we also know as Bathsheba, with whom King David committed adultery. The next part of Matthew's story begins with another young woman becoming pregnant through extraordinary circumstances as God continues to work toward the fulfillment of his ancient promises.

It's hard for us to imagine what the ancient Israelites' longing for their King, their Messiah, their long-expected anointed one, would have been like, but we will spend the following days this week looking at this aspect of Advent from the past. As we remember their waiting for the King's birth, and engage in the practices of waiting on him now, we will be better prepared for his return.

A Prayer for the Day:

O God, the King eternal, whose light divides the day from the night and turns the shadow of death into the morning: Drive far from us all wrong desires, incline our hearts to keep your law, and guide our feet into the way of peace; that, having done your will with cheerfulness while it was day, we may, when night comes, rejoice to give you thanks; through Jesus Christ our Lord. Amen.

A Prayer for the Week:

Stir up your power, O Lord, and with great might come among us; and, because we are sorely hindered by our sins, let your bountiful grace and mercy speedily help and deliver us; through Jesus Christ our Lord, to whom, with you and the Holy Spirit, be honor and glory, now and for ever. Amen.

Israel's Longing for the Temple

TO THE ANCIENT JEWS, the Temple was the place where heaven and earth overlapped.[29] It was the place where they could meet with God and their assurance of his ongoing presence among them. The Temple's predecessor, the Tabernacle, was the center of Israel's life with God from the time of the Exodus and their journey through the wilderness. King David desired to build a permanent sanctuary for the whole nation, which would be God's home among his people, and his son, Solomon, completed the grandiose project.

N.T. Wright describes:

When Israel's God blessed people, he did so from Zion [the location of the Temple]. When they were far away, they would turn and pray toward the Temple. When pilgrims and worshippers went up to Jerusalem and into the Temple to worship and offer sacrifices, they wouldn't have said that it was as though they were going into heaven. They would have said that they were going to the place where heaven and earth overlapped and interlocked.[30]

Understanding that the Temple was God's dwelling place helps us to understand the devastation so often expressed in the portions of the Old Testament written after the Babylonian exile, since the Temple was destroyed by the pagan Babylonians in 587 BC. Psalm 79 laments,

O God, the nations have come into your inheritance;
they have defiled your holy temple;
they have laid Jerusalem in ruins.
They have given the bodies of your servants
to the birds of the air for food,
the flesh of your faithful to the wild animals of the earth.
They have poured out their blood like water
all around Jerusalem,
and there was no one to bury them.
We have become a taunt to our neighbors,
mocked and derided by those around us.

How long, O LORD? Will you be angry forever?[31]

Rebuilding of the Temple began in 538 BC, and was completed in 516 BC, though it never matched the magnificence of its predecessor. Just as there was a sense in which Israel felt it had never fully returned from exile because they were continuously under the oppression of pagan empires, there was a sense in which God had never fully returned to dwell again in his Temple.

A little more than a decade before Jesus' birth, Herod the Great began to renovate, reconstruct, expand, and beautify the Temple. Though Herod had no royal blood, but was more like a warlord whom the Romans gave the title "King of the Jews," perhaps he understood something that had been passed down through all of the generations since King David: it was the king's job to build or restore the Temple and assure that God's people had access to the place where heaven and earth overlapped.

Wright notes: "The principle was established. Part of the central task of the king, should a true king ever emerge, would not only be to establish justice in the world; it would also involve the proper reestablishment of the place where heaven and earth met. The deep human longing for spirituality, for access, to God, would be answered at last."[32]

And so, by the time Jesus was born, almost six hundred years had passed while at least some of the people longed for the Temple to once again have its proper place in their life as a nation. Yet their efforts continually proved incomplete and Herod could build a magnificent building, but he was not and had no intention of being what the Scriptures called for Israel's true king to be.

So Israel longed and waited for their Temple, their place where heaven and earth overlapped, and they longed for their Messiah to come and establish it forever.

A Prayer for the Day:

O God, the author of peace and lover of concord, to know you is eternal life and to serve you is perfect freedom: Defend us, your humble servants, in all assaults of our enemies; that we, surely trusting in your defense, may not fear the power of any adversaries; through the might of Jesus Christ our Lord. Amen.

A Prayer for the Week:

Stir up your power, O Lord, and with great might come among us; and, because we are sorely hindered by our sins, let your bountiful grace and mercy speedily help and deliver us; through Jesus Christ our Lord, to whom, with you and the Holy Spirit, be honor and glory, now and for ever. Amen.

Israel's Longing for the Torah

AS WE HAVE SEEN, by the time of Jesus' birth, many of the Jews of his day were longing for their true King (their "anointed one"/Messiah/Christ) to come. When he came, he—as a descendant of David—would fulfill God's promises that David and Solomon would always have an heir as King of Israel. Following their long exile and oppression, the King would deliver Israel from their oppressors and enable them to once again truly be Israel. Once this Messiah would free them from their tyrants, he would enable them to become a true, faithful Israel by reestablishing the Temple as well as by giving the Torah its rightful central place in their life as a people.

It's virtually impossible for us to comprehend how much the Torah (the Law of Moses) mattered to many Jews in Jesus' day. It gave them the story of who they were: the descendants of Abraham, Isaac, and Jacob who had been enslaved in Egypt before being rescued by God and brought into the promised land. In their years there, however, they often failed to observe the law, and—as the Torah itself predicted—disaster came. The Temple was destroyed and the freedom God had given them from slavery disappeared as they went into exile.

We often mischaracterize the Torah as if it were simply God's way of setting a perfect standard no one would be able to reach through several centuries before eventually he would relent and make mercy and forgiveness available to us. While the Torah often did set high standards, that wasn't the point. It wasn't that God gave the Torah in the Old Testament as an experiment (which he knew would fail) in which people were required to attempt to earn their right standing with God. Rather, it was a pattern of life by which the people whom God rescued could show their gratitude, loyalty, and determination to live by the covenant because of which God rescued them in the first place.[33]

There were periods of Israel's history through which the Torah was not widely known and observed, and many of the writings during the exile look back and say, "We have failed to live God's way, and this is why this tragedy has happened to us." As we read through the biblical accounts of the generations from David until the exile, one person in each generation is given more of the weight of responsibility for the entire nation's observance of the Torah than anyone else: the King. Until the exile, the books of Kings and Chronicles largely judge the success or failure of each king's rule by the Torah: did he do what God commanded or did he disobey, and did he lead the people to observe God's law or to stray from it?

With the wounds of exile and six centuries of oppression always before them, many of the Jews of Jesus' day had become painstakingly scrupulous in their study and observance of the Torah. It was part of their longing for God to set things right. As they waited and observed God's law, it was another dimension of their yearning for the true King to come. He would deliver them from the pagans who didn't know the Torah, didn't care about the Temple, and often forced the Jews to disobey God's law. In contrast to their foolish kings who led them into exile, the long-awaited Messiah would fulfill the Torah himself and enable all of them to do so as well.

As with the other parts of their longing we have considered this week, their hopes were going to be fulfilled, but the King who was drawing near to them would meet their longings in radically different ways than they could have envisioned.

A Prayer for the Day:

Lord God, almighty and everlasting Father, you have brought us in safety to this new day: Preserve us with your mighty power, that we may not fall into sin, nor be overcome by adversity; and in all we do, direct us to the fulfilling of your purpose; through Jesus Christ our Lord. Amen.

A Prayer for the Week:

Stir up your power, O Lord, and with great might come among us; and, because we are sorely hindered by our sins, let your bountiful grace and mercy speedily help and deliver us; through Jesus Christ our Lord, to whom, with you and the Holy Spirit, be honor and glory, now and for ever. Amen.

Israel's Longing for New Creation

L AST WEEK, A FRIEND OF MINE from college lost his wife to pancreatic cancer. She was thirty-six, and leaves behind a loving husband and four young children grieving her loss. Her funeral service is happening as I write these words, and I can't help but wish that I could take over some of the burden of grief for them. It just isn't right that they had to lose her in this way.

About six weeks ago, a massive typhoon hit the Philippines, killing more than 6,000 people. The images of the devastation were overwhelming. Because of the speed of our media communications, every time a natural disaster hits, we can either become overwhelmed with the images of suffering on our TV and computer screens, or we can become calloused to it and attempt to shrug it off. Either way, we all have a sense that it isn't right that our world is like this.

Those examples don't even mention the horrible things we do to each other, and since our theme for this week is the yearning of Israel that we remember during Advent, I would be remiss not to lament the suffering of the Jewish people in both ancient and modern times. The Jews are so well-acquainted with the cry of "How long can our world be like this," that we Christians should recognize that we are following their lead whenever we offer any similar prayer.

If, as I said earlier this week, we must understand the thoroughly Jewish story in which Jesus lived if we are going to have any chance of understanding him, it's also surely the case that to really grasp our longing for his return, we have to look for its framework in Israel's yearning for their true King to come. While not presuming that I can equate the griefs I have experienced in my life with the tremendous suffering of the Jewish people throughout the centuries, I think it's good for us to realize that we have inherited our "How long, O Lord?" prayer from them.

The Hebrew Scriptures are full of that prayer in many different forms, and they also contain the vision of what the world will be like when God finally does set everything right, so today I'd like to let some of the greatest passages largely speak for themselves. In the book of Isaiah, which we are given to read often during Advent, we read both about ancient Israel's lament of how their world was and the hope that God would make things right, and Isaiah particularly emphasizes the point that everything would be made right not only for Israel, but indeed for the whole world and all of creation. Consider these examples from some of the traditional Advent readings from Isaiah:

He shall judge between the nations,
and shall arbitrate for many peoples;
they shall beat their swords into plowshares,
and their spears into pruning hooks;
nation shall not lift up sword against nation,
neither shall they learn war any more.[34]

The wilderness and the dry land shall be glad,
the desert shall rejoice and blossom....
Then the eyes of the blind shall be opened,
and the ears of the deaf unstopped;
then the lame shall leap like a deer,
and the tongue of the speechless sing for joy.
For waters shall break forth in the wilderness,

and streams in the desert;
the burning sand shall become a pool,
and the thirsty ground springs of water....
And the ransomed of the LORD *shall return,*
and come to Zion with singing;
everlasting joy shall be upon their heads;
they shall obtain joy and gladness,
and sorrow and sighing shall flee away.[35]

O that you would tear open the heavens and come down...
We have all become like one who is unclean,
and all our righteous deeds are like a filthy cloth.
We all fade like a leaf,
and our iniquities, like the wind, take us away.
There is no one who calls on your name,
or attempts to take hold of you;
for you have hidden your face from us,
and have delivered us into the hand of our iniquity.
Yet, O LORD, *you are our Father;*
we are the clay, and you are our potter;
we are all the work of your hand.
Do not be exceedingly angry, O LORD,
and do not remember iniquity forever.
Now consider, we are all your people.[36]

And in one of the magnificent concluding passages of the book:

For I am about to create new heavens
and a new earth;
the former things shall not be remembered
or come to mind.
But be glad and rejoice forever
in what I am creating;
for I am about to create Jerusalem as a joy,
and its people as a delight.
I will rejoice in Jerusalem,

and delight in my people;
no more shall the sound of weeping be heard in it,
or the cry of distress.
No more shall there be in it
an infant that lives but a few days,
or an old person who does not live out a lifetime;
for one who dies at a hundred years will be considered a youth,
and one who falls short of a hundred will be considered accursed.
They shall build houses and inhabit them;
they shall plant vineyards and eat their fruit.
They shall not build and another inhabit;
they shall not plant and another eat;
for like the days of a tree shall the days of my people be,
and my chosen shall long enjoy the work of their hands.
They shall not labor in vain,
or bear children for calamity;
for they shall be offspring blessed by the LORD—
and their descendants as well.
Before they call I will answer,
while they are yet speaking I will hear.
The wolf and the lamb shall feed together,
the lion shall eat straw like the ox;
but the serpent—its food shall be dust!
They shall not hurt or destroy
on all my holy mountain,
says the LORD.*"*[37]

Each time that we have grieved a tragedy and wished for a different kind of world, we have participated in Israel's longing for new creation. Even if we would never use those words, the sense that "this just is not right" is evidence that this yearning of God's people through the ages is deeply ingrained in us all.

Thankfully, Isaiah both acknowledges the reality of the pain and points us toward God's intervention. As we've seen the past couple of days with Israel's longing for the Temple and the Torah, the longing for new creation which we've inherited from the Old Testament is again tied to their longing for the coming of their real King, the Messiah. N.T. Wright points to the prophecy of Isaiah 11, which tells of how this descendant of Jesse and David "will bring restoration and healing to the whole world," since "this king will possess the wisdom he will need to bring God's justice to the whole world....The rule of the Messiah, then, will bring peace, justice, and a completely new harmony to the whole creation."[38]

"The spirit of the Lord shall rest on him, the spirit of wisdom and understanding, the spirit of counsel and might, the spirit of knowledge and the fear of the Lord. His delight shall be in the fear of the Lord. He shall not judge by what his eyes see, or decide by what his ears hear; but with righteousness he shall judge the poor, and decide with equity for the meek of the earth;

The wolf shall live with the lamb, the leopard shall lie down with the kid, the calf and the lion and the fatling together, and a little child shall lead them.

They will not hurt or destroy on all my holy mountain; for the earth will be full of the knowledge of the Lord as the waters cover the sea."[39]

A Prayer for the Day:

Heavenly Father, in you we live and move and have our being: We humbly pray you so to guide and govern us by your Holy Spirit, that in all the cares and occupations of our life we may not forget you, but may remember that we are ever walking in your sight; through Jesus Christ our Lord. Amen.

A Prayer for the Week:

Stir up your power, O Lord, and with great might come among us; and, because we are sorely hindered by our sins, let your bountiful grace and mercy speedily help and deliver us; through Jesus Christ our Lord, to whom, with you and the Holy Spirit, be honor and glory, now and for ever. Amen.

John's Cry in the Wilderness

ONE OF THE HIGHLIGHTS OF EACH YEAR for me is taking part in a camp meeting which my great-grandparents began attending in the early 1900s in the Davis Mountains of West Texas. We still live very close to the place where they settled more than a century ago, and the trip that used to take them a few days in a wagon now takes us about three hours in a nicely air-conditioned and smooth-riding vehicle. Part of the difference in the travel time now is obviously the faster vehicles we have in which to travel, but those vehicles wouldn't be of any use to us if it were not for the other major difference: roads. Life as it was a century ago without today's ease of transportation is difficult to imagine. I'll never know the names of the people who built the good roads through the mountains between here and our campground, but I'm very thankful that they did.

That image of preparing a road through difficult terrain is how each of the four gospels describes the work of one of the central characters of Advent: John the Baptist:

The word of God came to John son of Zechariah in the wilderness. He went into all the region around the Jordan, proclaiming a baptism of repentance for the forgiveness of sins, as it is written in the book of the words of the prophet Isaiah,

"The voice of one crying out in the wilderness:
'Prepare the way of the Lord,
make his paths straight.

Every valley shall be filled,
and every mountain and hill shall be made low,
and the crooked shall be made straight,
and the rough ways made smooth;
and all flesh shall see the salvation of God.'"[40]

In reading these words that the gospel writers chose to describe John, it should again be obvious to us that in order to understand John the Baptist and what he helps us to learn about Jesus, we have to get to know the story he lived in and see his place within it. Of course, as with Jesus, John lived within the story of ancient Israel. Also alike to Jesus, the writers of the gospels found help in Isaiah for understanding who John was and what he did.

Luke's quotation of Isaiah above comes from the first passage in Isaiah's second major section, chapters 40-55. Chapters 1-39 are sometimes referred to as Isaiah's "book of judgment," because it is full of warnings about the devastation that was coming to Israel if they continued to depart from God's commands. Chapter 40 begins a section sometimes called Isaiah's "book of comfort," because it comes to Israel after that devastation had come through their exile to Babylon and is full of promises of redemption and God's deliverance. This powerful section begins with these words:

Comfort, O comfort my people,
says your God.
Speak tenderly to Jerusalem,
and cry to her
that she has served her term,
that her penalty is paid,
that she has received from the LORD*'s hand*
double for all her sins.
A voice cries out:
"In the wilderness prepare the way of the LORD*,*
make straight in the desert a highway for our God."[41]

The destruction of Jerusalem and its Temple left the people of Judah with the sense that not only had God left the Temple and Jerusalem, but that God had abandoned them, and in their suffering, they were desperate for him to return and restore them. As we have seen already this week, this hope centered on the dream that their true King would emerge. He would come and deliver them from their oppressors. He would restore the place where heaven and earth overlapped in the Temple. He would be one who fulfilled the Torah and led the nation to do so as well. Then, Israel could fulfill its place in the world, bringing God's blessing to all nations and all of creation.

But how could all of that happen when God had seemingly abandoned them? The beginning of Isaiah's words of comfort indicated that God was indeed coming back to his people, but like preparing for an ancient king's return to a territory after a long absence, the roads through the mountains needed to be cleared. The way needed to be prepared for the king's arrival.

Around 600 years after the prophecy in Isaiah, Israel was still longing for their true King to come and be their deliverer. Herod was building a Temple, but it wasn't yet truly the place again where heaven and earth overlapped. God had not yet fully returned to them and rescued them from their suffering. They were becoming ever more diligent in scrupulously observing the Torah, but God's new world still seemed a distant reality.

It was during that time that a locust-eating, fur-wearing misfit in the desert began shouting his message that God was indeed about to return as King, and therefore, all of Israel needed to change their direction and prepare accordingly. Matthew, Mark, Luke, and John each saw this as fitting what Isaiah's first words of comfort had described so long before. God was coming—they needed to prepare the way and be ready.

John's call to repentance is an essential aspect of our Advent waiting which we haven't yet explored. He came saying that God's kingdom was near, meaning that the hope of their centuries of waiting was about to be fulfilled. It was right on the verge of being realized. Like the other centuries of followers of the King before us, we are urged to live each day realizing we are on the verge of his return. As we remember John's part of the story each Advent, we have to consider what we might do to prepare our own hearts and our world to welcome him when he comes.

A Prayer for the Day:

Almighty God, whose most dear Son went not up to joy but first he suffered pain, and entered not into glory before he was crucified: Mercifully grant that we, walking in the way of the cross, may find it none other than the way of life and peace; through Jesus Christ our Lord. Amen.

A Prayer for the Week:

Stir up your power, O Lord, and with great might come among us; and, because we are sorely hindered by our sins, let your bountiful grace and mercy speedily help and deliver us; through Jesus Christ our Lord, to whom, with you and the Holy Spirit, be honor and glory, now and for ever. Amen.

Habakkuk's Plea

A MONG THE BOOKS YOU AND I *don't* read to our families around a fireplace in December as a way of getting ready for Christmas is the three-chapter Old Testament book of Habakkuk. That's okay, because I would much rather sit with my children and watch Linus tell Charlie Brown and the *Peanuts* gang what Christmas is all about than I would read them this book in which God tells Habakkuk that he's preparing a devastation of Judah so astounding that it wouldn't be believable it even if he were told.

Yet while Habakkuk will never make a popular Christmas children's book or TV special, it is fitting for Advent as we have been exploring it together. (This fact alone should let me know that I shouldn't expect this Advent book to ever become a bestseller.) Particularly for this week, as we have explored ancient Israel's long period of waiting for the Messiah to come, I think it's helpful to listen to what Habakkuk had to say before we turn a corner into the final week of Advent.

Habakkuk's opening words characterize well the longing and waiting of Advent:

> O LORD, how long shall I cry for help,
> and you will not listen?
> Or cry to you "Violence!"
> and you will not save?[42]

Habakkuk is a book for all of the times when God's people have exclaimed, "This just isn't right!" and pled with God to do something about the broken world around us. God responds to some of Habakkuk's questions, but doesn't fully engage his complaints. Habakkuk laments things he sees daily: oppression and violence, indifference to God's law, and how God is seemingly unresponsive in spite of them.

Yet Habakkuk waits:

> *I will stand at my watchpost*
> *and station myself on the rampart;*
> *I will keep watch to see what he will say to me,*
> *and what he will answer concerning my complaint.* [43]

Then, after a list of the kinds of things that made Habakkuk yearn for God's intervention, he concludes:

> *But the LORD is in his holy temple;*
> *let all the earth keep silence before him!*[44]

As we bring to an end these three weeks of considering different aspects of waiting on God, it's appropriate for us to follow Habakkuk's example of how he (and surely many others in ancient Israel) waited on God: to lament over the abundance of brokenness in our world as it is, and then to realize that God is still not far off and to be quiet in the presence of the one who has promised us that he will indeed come and make all things new. If we can cultivate that sense of quietness in the midst of the swirling world around us, we will be ready to be attentive through next week's journey with those people in the biblical stories who were there to greet the Messiah. Silenced awe may be the best possible reaction once we finally arrive at the point of considering how a human baby could completely redefine what this means: God is in his holy temple.

A Prayer for the Day:

Almighty God, who after the creation of the world rested from all your works and sanctified a day of rest for all your creatures: Grant that we, putting away all earthly anxieties, may be duly prepared for the service of your sanctuary, and that our rest here upon earth may be a preparation for the eternal rest promised to your people in heaven; through Jesus Christ our Lord. Amen

A Prayer for the Week:

Stir up your power, O Lord, and with great might come among us; and, because we are sorely hindered by our sins, let your bountiful grace and mercy speedily help and deliver us; through Jesus Christ our Lord, to whom, with you and the Holy Spirit, be honor and glory, now and for ever. Amen.

A Note on Reading Through the Fourth Week of Advent

Because Christmas Day falls on different days of the week from year to year, the fourth week of Advent can have anywhere from one to seven days. Therefore, each of the readings in this final week can stand on its own, allowing you to use the appropriate number of days for whichever year you are reading.

As a result, if Christmas Eve is any day of the week other than Sunday, begin the week by reading "Fourth Sunday of Advent: Waiting Like Zechariah" on page 88. Then, on Monday, turn to the corresponding date between December 19 and 24.

If Christmas Eve is a Sunday this year, skip ahead to "Waiting Like Simeon" on page 113.

Waiting Like Zechariah

ERHAPS THE QUESTION MOST CHARACTERISTIC OF ADVENT is, "How long, O Lord?" It isn't a question that only comes up in a verse or two of Scripture, but it gets asked in various forms more than thirty times in the Bible. Take these examples, just from the Psalms:

> *How long, O LORD?*
> *Will you forget me forever?*
> *How long will you hide your face from me?*
> *How long must I bear pain in my soul,*
> *and have sorrow in my heart all day long?*
> *How long shall my enemy be exalted over me?*[45]

> *How long, O God, is the foe to scoff?*
> *Is the enemy to revile your name forever?*[46]

> *Turn, O LORD! How long?*
> *Have compassion on your servants!*[47]

> *How long must your servant endure?*
> *When will you judge those who persecute me?*[48]

We are certainly in good company when we ask the question of God, whether during Advent or any other time. Yet there is an accompanying version of the question that we should pose not to God, but to ourselves: How long are we willing to wait? How long will we remain faithful if it seems that God continually remains silent?

One reason that I'm pretty weak when it comes to waiting on God is that, while I think it's a good thing to wait through the kinds of practices we explored in the first week, I seem to have an unstated time limit on how long I'm willing to do so before I place my demands on God that he take notice and respond. That kind of limited waiting isn't really what it means to wait on God, because we still have things according to our own terms. On the other hand, when I think of the lives of those I've known who have had the kind of life with God I desire, they seemed to have developed an ability to wait on God without any limits, whether it meant months, years, decades, or even an entire lifetime.

Luke introduces us to a person like this in the beginning of his gospel:

> *In the days of King Herod of Judea, there was a priest named Zechariah, who belonged to the priestly order of Abijah. His wife was a descendant of Aaron, and her name was Elizabeth. Both of them were righteous before God, living blamelessly according to all the commandments and regulations of the Lord. But they had no children, because Elizabeth was barren, and both were getting on in years.*[49]

Being described as "righteous before God, living blamelessly according to all the commandments and regulations of the Lord" is high praise from Luke for Zechariah and Elizabeth. They had lived good, faithful lives before God, and they had done so for a very long time. Yet through decades of waiting on God through their prayers, their service, and their obedience, God had been silent. Elizabeth was barren in a culture in which that was considered a disgrace. God was not only quiet in regard to their personal struggles, but God's old promises to their ancestors continued to be unfulfilled. How could God bless all of the nations of the world through the family of Abraham when they were continually oppressed, generation after generation, by one brutal empire after another? Would the real heir to David's throne ever appear and deliver them?

In spite of their faithful waiting on God, God had left Zechariah, his family, and his people in a painful place for a very long time. Yet Zechariah continued to offer his prayers and wait, year after year, with no apparent reward.

How long are we willing to wait? How long will we remain faithful if it seems that God continually remains silent?

If we read through the remainder of the first chapter of Luke, we see how the angel Gabriel burst into Zechariah's normal routine of serving and waiting on God one day while he was giving the incense offering in the Temple. Zechariah was told that God had heard his prayer, and that he and Elizabeth would have a son whom they were to name John. Zechariah may have been devoted and faithful, but he still didn't find difficult things easy to believe, and thus he was unable to speak from that day until the promised son was born, when Zechariah shocked his friends and neighbors by writing on a tablet and insisting, "His name is John."

We can see a parallel between Zechariah's silence while waiting for John's birth and what was happening in Israel at the time: God and his prophets had seemingly been silent—not just for the term of a pregnancy, but for centuries. But now, at the birth of a baby, God's word was about to come again in unprecedented and unforeseen ways.[50]

Upon the baby's birth and naming, Zechariah regained his ability to speak and gave a prophecy of his own which Christians through the ages have found worth repetitive reflection for increasing our understanding of who both John and Jesus were and what they did. It's found in Luke 1:67-79, and is worth stopping to read now if you're able.

It's a remarkable vision of what God was about to do through these two baby boys, and it reflects how Israel's long period of yearning for their King was about to be met. It says that the old promises of God to his people were about to be fulfilled, that they would be delivered by a descendant of David, and it also points to ways in which the deliverance will extend beyond political freedom, even reaching into the shadow of death itself:

Blessed be the Lord God of Israel...
He has raised up a mighty savior for us
in the house of his servant David...
that we would be saved from our enemies
and from the hand of all who hate us.
...[He has remembered] the oath that he swore
to our ancestor Abraham, to grant us that we,
being rescued from the hands of our enemies,
might serve him without fear, in holiness and righteousness
before him all our days.
...By the tender mercy of our God,
the dawn from on high will break upon us,
to give light to those who sit in darkness
and in the shadow of death,
to guide our feet into the way of peace.[51]

For our Advent waiting, it's also helpful to consider what Zechariah's words reveal, not only about John and Jesus, but also about Zechariah himself and how he became the kind of person who could wait on God with such faithfulness throughout his life. Along with what Luke had already mentioned about Zechariah's consistency in the face of God's silence, the words of this prophecy also reveal the depth to which Zechariah had studied and pondered the Hebrew Scriptures. He knew the story in which these two boys were going to play major roles, and it's a safe assumption for us to think that the depth to which he had reflected on the Scriptures formed the substance of his ability to continue to hope in the midst of God's silence in his own life, plus the centuries of agony of his own people.

So, we can wait like Zechariah by doing the kinds of things he did: praying, soaking our minds in the Scripture's story of how God has worked throughout history, and letting that story shape our hope regardless of how long God seems to be silent. Wright describes Zechariah's example well: "God regularly works through ordinary people, doing what they normally do, who with a mixture of half-faith and devotion are holding themselves ready for whatever God has in mind."[52]

A Prayer for the Day:

O God, you make us glad with the weekly remembrance of the glorious resurrection of your Son our Lord: Give us this day such blessing through our worship of you, that the week to come may be spent in your favor; through Jesus Christ our Lord. Amen.

A Prayer for the Week:

Purify our conscience, Almighty God, by your daily visitation, that your Son Jesus Christ, at his coming, may find in us a mansion prepared for himself; who lives and reigns with you, in the unity of the Holy Spirit, one God, now and for ever. Amen.

Waiting Like Abraham

I AM HEREBY LOBBYING FOR ABRAHAM to be included in our nativity sets. I admit it would be a little strange, since he lived about as many centuries before Jesus' birth as we do after it, and therefore including him would make as much historical sense as including a figurine of LeBron James. Nevertheless, historical accuracy isn't what we are after in those sets anyway. If it were, for starters, there would be no wise men (since they didn't come along until Jesus was a toddler when the family lived in a house), no livestock (there isn't any mention of them at all), and no barn (more likely, a cave or lower part of a relative's house). So, since we apparently either aren't interested in recreating the historical scene or don't know any better, why not include Abraham?

Zechariah mentioned Abraham in connection with Jesus' birth[53], so that's a point in favor of my cause. For that matter, even Mary mentioned Abraham in connection with Jesus' birth[54], and don't you think that, of all people, *she* should get to decide whom to invite to this party?

The fact that Abraham had been dead for about two millennia when Joseph and Mary came to Bethlehem has heretofore been [unjustly] sufficient to exclude him from the cast of Christmas characters, but since this book is about Advent—about waiting on God—there's no one who has been more obviously ostracized than Abraham. Even if I can't convince any nativity set manufacturers to add an Abrahamic figurine, I'll do my best to put him in his rightful place in our attention in these final days before Christmas.

I'm not lobbying for Abraham's case just because he has an irreplaceable role in the story that led up to that night in Bethlehem, even though that's true. If you remember our exploration last week of Matthew's genealogy about Jesus, you'll recall that as Matthew tells it, the first name in the story that led to Jesus was the name of Abraham. Jesus' story is inevitably a story about the descendants of Abraham.

I'm also not lobbying his case just because the ways he had to wait on God during his lifetime are very instructive for us, even though that's true and remarkable. Anyone who saw God's promise of a son being born come true at age one hundred (twenty-five years after God promised it!) would be worth listening to on the topic of waiting. It would be fascinating to hear Abraham as the keynote speaker on waiting, partly because of how often he did a poor job of it. As much as having something to say about passing the century mark before his wife had a son, he might have as much to say about the times when he took things into his own hands, apparently in case God's promises needed some help in coming to fruition.

No, my motive for including Abraham as a central character in our considerations of Advent is because of his willingness to wait for things even beyond his own lifetime. In addition to the birth of a son, God also promised Abraham innumerable descendants, possession of land, and that all the peoples of the earth would be blessed through him.

As we discussed on Sunday, we're in good company when we ask the "How long, O Lord?" question of God. However, the accompanying question to us is: How long are we willing to wait? How long will we remain faithful if it seems that God continually remains silent?

Abraham was seventy-five years old and childless when God said to him, "I will make of you a great nation...and in you all the families of the earth shall be blessed." He waited another quarter-century before the birth of the son God promised. Even as miraculous as the birth of that son was, by the time of Abraham's death (after *another* seventy-five years!), how many of the promises that God made seemed to be coming true?

Old Testament scholar Victor Hamilton notes,

What about Abraham? He has a son, or two, but not a myriad of descendants. He has a tent and wealth, but no land, except for the purchase of a tiny bit of property on which to bury his wife. And during the last seventy-five years of his life, how many families of the earth are blessed in him?

One rich blessing Abraham has. True, he does not have, in terms of personal realization, all the promises of God. But he does have the God of all the promises....The giver, and not the gifts, is Abraham's highest reward and his consuming obsession. Not without reason, therefore, is Abraham referred to three times in the Bible as "the friend of God." They enjoyed each other's company.[55]

In other words, if we could get Abraham to give a keynote address, or perhaps to write a preface for one of the "God's Promises" kind of books always available in Christian bookstores, I'm pretty sure he would include something along the lines of, *You can wait all you want, but won't live to see most of those promises come true. Are you okay with that?*

Well, are you?

Often, I can't answer yes. I may be willing to wait on God for a week, perhaps even throughout the duration of Advent. Abraham's quarter-century would be pushing things drastically for me, but I think I have an unspoken expectation that God needs to live up to anything he's said while I'm still around to see it. I'm willing to wait on God, but circumstances have a way of revealing the limits I put on that willingness.

Jesus got himself into trouble with a strange comment about Abraham. Near the end of a heated discussion with some religious leaders who felt their authority threatened by Jesus, he said,

> *"Your ancestor Abraham rejoiced that he would see my day; he saw it and was glad." Then the Jews said to him, "You are not yet fifty years old, and have you seen Abraham?" Jesus said to them, "Very truly, I tell you, before Abraham was, I am." So they picked up stones to throw at him, but Jesus hid himself and went out of the temple.*[56]

Abraham knew God. He trusted God. He, who died with two sons (but only one of whom he had seen during the past seventy-five years), was a friend of the great I AM who told him that nations would come from his countless descendants. He could look forward to the fulfillment of God's promises—regardless of how many millennia would be required—because Abraham wasn't sustained by promises that could happen well beyond his lifetime. Rather than being upheld by God's promises, it was God's presence that gave Abraham the strength he needed.

Waiting requires fortitude and endurance, and Abraham teaches us that anyone willing to wait on God longer than their own lifetime can only do so by being with God long enough to learn to enjoy one another's company.

A Prayer for the Week:

Purify our conscience, Almighty God, by your daily visitation, that your Son Jesus Christ, at his coming, may find in us a mansion prepared for himself; who lives and reigns with you, in the unity of the Holy Spirit, one God, now and for ever. Amen.

December 20

Waiting Like Joseph

MY MARRIAGE TO MY WONDERFUL WIFE, KARA, has been the most deeply satisfying experience of my life. I am inexpressibly grateful for my life with her—particularly when I think back to how close our marriage came to not happening.

We began dating during our senior year of college at Asbury University, which meant that after about six months of dating, we began a long-distance relationship. She stayed in Kentucky, I moved to Georgia, and we did the best we could in those days before cell phones were common. Enduring the geographical distance wasn't fun, and I clearly remember saying goodbye to her at the end of one of our visits and then heading straight to the store to purchase a ring. I couldn't stand the distance any longer.

I don't remember how many weeks there were between the time that I bought that ring and when I got to see her again, but time passes very slowly for a boy who has paid for an engagement ring but not yet had an opportunity to put it on the finger of the one for whom it was purchased. In the meantime, I concocted a plan, rehearsed what I wanted to say, and then eventually bought some roses and hit the road to pop the question.

There is much that I don't remember about what happened after I arrived, but even though I'm not always very good at reading signals, my first major clue that the ring burning a hole in my pocket was going to have to stay there longer than I thought was when she said, "I think we should take a break [from dating each other] for a while."

Whatever it was that happened following that comment has been blocked out of my memory, though apparently it was impossible for me to hide my angst for the rest of the evening. I must have been making my distress obvious enough that, finally, she dug it out of me, imploring me to tell her what was wrong. I couldn't avoid the issue any longer and told her, "I was going to propose to you."

By that time, my proposal plan was down the tubes, the relationship felt in jeopardy, and I still had a shiny ring in my pocket that I didn't know what to do with. By God's grace, somewhere after all of that confusion, she told me something like, "I changed my mind about wanting a break. I really do want to marry you." I then tried my best to get her to go with me to my planned proposal spot in the hopes that the roses I'd ordered might still show up, and I clearly remember kicking the wall when they weren't there. Later that night, I found a much less romantic way to propose than either of us had hoped for, and thankfully—she indeed had changed her mind, and did say yes. The quality of our life together since then has more than made up for the lack of quality of our engagement experience.

I tell that somewhat embarrassing story, not because I'm going to pretend to have any inkling of a clue as to what Joseph's experience was like, but to point out how much more deeply wrenched his guts must have felt when he learned that his Mary was pregnant. Obviously, that was a much more drastic halting of their plans than when I was told my girlfriend wanted to take a break for a while. Just as Joseph's years of waiting for a wife were about to end, she was pregnant. I can't imagine how deeply hurt and angry he must have been.

Thankfully, God intervened by sending an angel to Joseph in a dream to assure him he did not need to be afraid to take Mary as his wife, and that the child she was carrying was from the Holy Spirit.

We aren't given much information about Joseph in the Bible. We have a list of his ancestors. We learn later than he was a carpenter and was no longer alive when Jesus was an adult. Matthew describes Joseph as a righteous man, and he obeyed what God told him to do. Whereas Luke's telling of the Christmas story focuses on Mary and her extraordinary openness to God, Matthew tells the story with more of an emphasis on Joseph's unremarkable reluctance.

And that's about the entirety of the picture we're given of him. He did what was right, and once he had a family, he was protective of them.

I wonder what the months in between Joseph's dream and Jesus' birth were like. Pregnancy alone teaches mothers about waiting in ways valuable enough that perhaps they should be writing this book instead of me, but before we look at the unmatched ways that Mary waited on God, it's good to consider how Joseph's waiting was also unique. He was told that the coming child was the one who would save God's people from their sins, so surely Joseph waited in awe, all along knowing both that God had given him a great responsibility and that the child coming wasn't his.

Joseph's waiting challenges me because the part God gave him to play was one of doing the right, loving thing and then disappearing from history. It wouldn't be for a few more decades that the family's nephew, John, would gain a following as a desert prophet and would say about Jesus, "He must increase; I must decrease," but by the time that John said those words, Joseph had already lived them.

Joseph made a habit of doing the right thing while he waited on God, and then he died. May such simple but difficult words be said about each of us when our days are through.

A Prayer for the Day:

O God, who from the family of your servant David raised up Joseph to be the guardian of your incarnate Son and the spouse of his virgin mother: Give us grace to imitate his uprightness of life and his obedience to your commands; through Jesus Christ our Lord, who lives and reigns with you and the Holy Spirit, one God, for ever and ever. Amen.

A Prayer for the Week:

Purify our conscience, Almighty God, by your daily visitation, that your Son Jesus Christ, at his coming, may find in us a mansion prepared for himself; who lives and reigns with you, in the unity of the Holy Spirit, one God, now and for ever. Amen.

Waiting Like Shepherds

IT APPEARS THAT THE GOD OF THE BIBLE has a disproportionate fondness for shepherds. That's the only reason I can see why a group of them were privileged enough to be the ones to receive the news of the Messiah's birth, and to be invited to go lay eyes on the newborn king. In thinking, however, about their waiting prior to that stunning angelic announcement, my mind goes to how low shepherds always ranked on the pecking orders of the world and how incommensurately often God's affection for them was put on display.

Genesis doesn't say why God accepted Abel's offering from among his flocks while disapproving of Cain's crops, but perhaps that was the first Biblical occurrence in the pattern of the Almighty's attachment to shepherds. Out of the mess that the world had become from the time of Cain and Abel's parents through the next twenty generations, God finally chose someone through whom he would begin to reconcile the world to himself—a shepherd to whom he would give the name Abraham.

Shepherding remained the family business for Abraham's descendants for some time, as this somewhat unduly favored family wrestled with God and one another, repeatedly took matters into their own hands, and yet were constantly reminded that God was with them. Eventually they became slaves of the shepherd-despising Egyptians until God got the attention of a herdsman by speaking through a burning bush.

Moses then reluctantly went from tending sheep in the wilderness to ushering God's people out of oppression as God's people were led "like a flock by the hand of Moses and Aaron."[57]

About a half-millennium later, Israel's first king, Saul, was defying God's commands. God then bypassed more obvious choices for Saul's successor in order to call in a young boy, David, from tending sheep in the fields to return to Bethlehem and be anointed to lead God's people. At the end of David's life, God gave him a reminder and a promise: "I took you from the pasture, from following the sheep to be prince over my people Israel....your throne shall be established forever."[58]

Many of David's successors, however, led the people astray rather than continuing in the ways of God. Israel's psalmists and prophets came to describe this as a massive failure of these pseudo-shepherds and made their appeal to God:

Give ear, O Shepherd of Israel,
you who lead Joseph like a flock!
Stir up your might,
and come to save us!
Restore us, O God;
let your face shine, that we may be saved.[59]

When the group of shepherds near Bethlehem were addressed by the angels of God on the night of Jesus' birth, they had no qualifications whatsoever for being the first ones to be let in on Mary and Joseph's secret, the first ones to pay homage to the king. In no way had they earned that honor. We have no indication whether or not they were waiting on God in any purposeful ways. Apparently, the only reason they were given an invitation to find a baby in a manger was because God had a fondness for them and a pattern of undeservedly inviting shepherds into his most important moments of intervention on behalf of his people.

When those shepherds gazed at the face of that baby, perhaps they understood that they were in the presence of royalty, since they had been told he was the Messiah. However, they had no way of knowing how deeply this infant-King would one day identify himself with them: "I am the good shepherd. The good shepherd lays down his life for the sheep."[60] He would commission Peter with the words, "Tend my sheep."[61] His earliest followers would describe him as "the lamb of God who takes away the sins of the world"[62] and "our Lord Jesus, the great shepherd of the sheep."[63] Revelation mixes the two powerful metaphors into one: "...the Lamb at the center of the throne will be their shepherd, and he will guide them to springs of the water of life, and God will wipe away every tear from their eyes."[64]

It seems that throughout the Bible, God never decreased his fondness for shepherds. Though it seems strange to the rest of us, it seems like a fit that God would invite some of them to greet the one who would be both the good shepherd and the ultimate lamb.

Part of the good news of all of this for us is that—if God is so partial to shepherds and their sheep, and all of these shepherds had done nothing to merit their inclusion in God's plans—we can rest assured of God's fondness for us. In a few days, when we celebrate and sing, "O come, let us adore him," may we all be reminded that the invitation has come our way out of God's pure mercy and never-ending love for us.

A Prayer for the Week:

Purify our conscience, Almighty God, by your daily visitation, that your Son Jesus Christ, at his coming, may find in us a mansion prepared for himself; who lives and reigns with you, in the unity of the Holy Spirit, one God, now and for ever. Amen.

Waiting Like Wise Men

CAN JESUS BE WORSHIPPED BY MUSLIMS? I don't just mean people of Muslim descent who have converted to Christianity, but rather—can Jesus be worshipped by people in Islamic communities, who are participating in their mosques, who still identify themselves as Muslims rather than as Christians?

The January 2013 edition of *Christianity Today* was titled "Worshipping Jesus in the Mosque," and included stories of people who claim to be doing precisely what I described in the paragraph above. Predictably, it caused a stir. So, the more general question could be: Can those who do not claim to be part of the Christian religion genuinely worship Jesus?

If that question bothers you, perhaps you'll want to write it on a notecard, place it in the storage box for your nativity set's figurines and see what you think about it each year when you pull out those three images of pagan astrologers (a.k.a. the wise men) to display on your mantle alongside the Jewish baby and his Jewish parents.

These wise men come into Matthew's account of Jesus' birth about as tamely as an electric shock, but our Christmas cards and nativity sets have mellowed them to the extent that we no longer notice their jolt. (By the way, I don't think you need to do this but, if you're interested in making your Christmas celebration this year a bit more congruent with the biblical stories of Jesus' birth, the most obvious change you can make is to remove the wise men from your nativity set. Nothing in the Bible indicates that they were kings, nor that there were three of them, nor that they were present to see Jesus in a manger.)

Matthew's gospel is thoroughly Jewish—clearly written by a devoutly Jewish author and intended for a primarily Jewish audience. Yet immediately after writing about Jesus' birth, the gospel introduces these magi, apparently professional astrologers, who have deduced from the signs in their night sky that a new king has been born to the Jews. The inescapable irony here is that a) they're right, and b) the Jews would never have approved of their astrology and regarded it as a pagan practice.

To again attempt a more modern equivalent of the surprise of the situation, the pagan astrologers' ability to locate the newborn Jewish Messiah (which no Jewish person had been able to do) would be about as expected as walking into your church for worship—let's say on Easter Sunday—and being inspired by the finest sermon on Jesus' resurrection that you've ever heard...this time, from a Buddhist monk.

Those wise men didn't fit within the paradigms of any early hearer of Matthew's story. They were the wrong people, with misguided beliefs, who got their information in inappropriate ways...and it all led them (alone) to the Messiah. Matthew doesn't shy away from saying that they recognized him as the king of the Jews, and they acted accordingly when they saw him.

That's hard for me to wrap my mind around. Like virtually everyone else, I assume that I have it right—that my schemas of how the world works and what God is like are reasonably accurate. Yet it appears that God is bigger than our schemas. It appears that God's work through the Messiah born in Bethlehem was bigger than any ethnic or religious limitations.

I come from a family with a rich Christian heritage, and live in an area of the world where the vast majority of people identify themselves as Christians. But the shock of this story about the wise men is that I have to be humble enough to recognize that my pedigree doesn't preclude the possibility that there might be someone who has all of the "wrong" qualifications by "our" standards who nonetheless could have a much more accurate view of how *my* God is working in the world than I do—and they could be arranging the pursuits of their lives accordingly, just as the wise men did. As a pastor friend of mine once said in a sermon that caused someone to walk out and never enter back into his church, "Christianity is not the way—*Christ* is the way."[65] (Don't miss his point—the argument is not against Christianity, bur rather that Christ is larger than even our religious efforts.)

So how does the shock of the wise men inform our intent of waiting on God during these weeks of preparing our souls for Christmas? First, I think we need to recognize that God's grace toward us and toward every human being is bigger than we can grasp. God is working in the hearts and lives of every single person on the planet—including those whom we deem in the right circles and those we place in the wrong ones. The infant King whose birth we will soon celebrate is not our possession. He is King of the world.

Second, as we have emphasized repeatedly throughout these four weeks, we need to *know* him. Jesus explained to his disciples,

> *I am the good shepherd. I know my own and my own know me, just as the Father knows me and I know the Father. And I lay down my life for the sheep. I have other sheep that do not belong to this fold. I must bring them also, and they will listen to my voice. So there will be one flock, one shepherd.*[66]

Finally, I have said things in this entry about which I'm sincere, and knew that in doing so I would most likely challenge your thinking. I have not, however, said some things that could be read into my words—I haven't said that all religions are equal, nor that it's fine to like Jesus but not

Christianity. Rather, I believe that Jesus is King of us all and that the ways that God works tend to exceed whatever boundaries we may have come to expect. The question, therefore, is: when that happens, will we know him well enough to recognize God's work outside the bounds of where we thought it would be?

A Prayer for the Week:

Purify our conscience, Almighty God, by your daily visitation, that your Son Jesus Christ, at his coming, may find in us a mansion prepared for himself; who lives and reigns with you, in the unity of the Holy Spirit, one God, now and for ever. Amen.

Waiting Like Mary

I SAW MEL GIBSON'S *The Passion of the Christ* soon after it was released in 2004, and I clearly remember having a reaction which I never expected. There was a lot of hype surrounding the movie, and people were having a wide variety of reactions to it by the time I saw the film. Yet of all the comments I was hearing from friends or the media, no one was expressing the impact of the poignant scenes that are still in my mind today—the scenes that included Mary. No one else in history has ever had a role like Mary's, and many of my fellow Protestants and I have paid far too little attention to her. Any of us would certainly benefit tremendously from following her example of humble openness to God, regardless of which Christian tradition we call home.

Mary's uniqueness should have been obvious to me ever since I began to read the Bible, but it took the film's portrayal of Mary, including scenes from different stages of Jesus' life (from her caring for him as a young boy to her presence at his crucifixion), to bring my prior disregard of Jesus' mother to my attention.

There are many other Biblical characters in whose place I can imagine myself, but I can't do it with Mary. Perhaps some of that reason is due to me being a man and my total unfamiliarity with what it's like to have any kind of child growing inside of me—not to mention if that child happened to be God incarnate. But my inability to imagine myself in Mary's place in the stories goes deeper than the nature of our genders. There simply could never be another person to have had the role in Jesus' life that she had, nor to be impacted by him in the ways that she was. In other words, as one powerful scene of Gibson's film portrays, no one else who saw Jesus bleed on Calvary could have had flashbacks to picking him up as a toddler and caring for his scraped knee.

As worthy of our consideration as any of the parts of Jesus' and Mary's story are, here near the end of Advent, with Christmas approaching soon, we need to consider the way that only Mary waited on God, and what her waiting can teach the rest of us.

Luke's gospel gives us the fullest description of Mary's waiting, and part of the way he does so is to contrast her with the character we considered on Sunday, Zechariah. The story of Gabriel's visit to Zechariah in the Temple is followed immediately by the story of Gabriel's visit to Mary in Nazareth. Even though Zechariah was described as being righteous and blameless, Luke doesn't portray him as a hero, but rather with the kind of confused and baffled response to God's message through Gabriel that most of us might have had. The news was hard to believe, so Zechariah said he needed a sign to know that it was from God. Mary, on the other hand, responds with absolute humility and obedience. She too asked a question of Gabriel, but she asked for more information, rather than for proof.[67]

Zechariah thought Gabriel's message was impossible, asked for a sign, and ended up unable to speak until his son was born. Mary thought Gabriel's message was improbable but responded in humble obedience and ended up praising God through words that have been prayed, sung, studied, and meditated upon by Christians for two millennia:

My soul magnifies the Lord,
and my spirit rejoices in God my Savior,
for he has looked with favor on the lowliness of his servant.
Surely, from now on all generations will call me blessed;

for the Mighty One has done great things for me,
and holy is his name.
His mercy is for those who fear him
from generation to generation.
He has shown strength with his arm;
he has scattered the proud in the thoughts of their hearts.
He has brought down the powerful from their thrones,
and lifted up the lowly;
he has filled the hungry with good things,
and sent the rich away empty.
He has helped his servant Israel,
in remembrance of his mercy,
according to the promise he made to our ancestors,
to Abraham and to his descendants forever.[68]

In considering the profound way in which Mary waited for Jesus' coming, her song again reveals an inescapable aspect of learning to wait well. We saw it previously in Zechariah and will see it again in our character tomorrow: Mary had soaked her mind in the Scripture and the story revealed there of how God was working in human history. While perhaps we could naturally expect a high degree of scriptural literacy from Zechariah since he was a priest and had served God faithfully for a lifetime, our expectations of peasant teenage girls isn't quite so high. Yet it appears that not only had Mary absorbed the message of the Hebrew Scriptures, but that she had particularly set her mind upon the story of another remarkable mother in Israel's history, Hannah. The similarities between Mary's song and Hannah's prayer are striking:

My heart exults in the LORD;
my strength is exalted in my God.
...Those who were full have hired themselves out for bread,
but those who were hungry are fat with spoil.
...The LORD makes poor and makes rich;
he brings low, he also exalts.
He raises up the poor from the dust;

he lifts the needy from the ash heap,
to make them sit with princes
and inherit a seat of honor. [69]

Mary was able to wait on God by responding in humility ("Here am I, the servant of the Lord; let it be with me according to your word."), and by having already soaked her mind in the Scripture. Also, before moving on, we do Mary's example injustice if we fail to consider the *bodily*, physical, very human nature of her obedience to God. We too often think that if we are to live the kind of life that would be pleasing to God—or even just to wait on God during Advent or celebrate Christmas well—that it would primarily be something "spiritual" and we rarely if ever consider the irreplaceable role that our bodies have in our lives with God. Mary, however, didn't have the opportunity to make such a mistake since what God was asking of her involved her body to the furthest possible extent.

If you and I have the courage and humility to experiment with praying Mary's prayer ("Here am I, the servant of the Lord; let it be with me according to your word.), we will also find that our bodies are always included if we are to follow through in obedience. We will be given opportunities to praise God with our mouths, love people with our hands and feet, study with our eyes, and worship with every part of us. In other words, we will be asked—as Mary was—to wait on God by allowing the Messiah to dwell *in* us, so that our bodily lives may bring his blessing to those around us.

As you enter into this final time of preparation for Christmas, what is one way today that you can wait like Mary and open the deepest parts of your life to the one who says, "Abide in me, and I will abide in you"?

A Prayer for the Day:

Father in heaven, by your grace the virgin mother of your incarnate Son was blessed in bearing him, but still more blessed in keeping your word: Grant us who honor the exaltation of her lowliness to follow the example of her devotion to your will; through Jesus Christ our Lord, who lives and reigns with you and the Holy Spirit, one God, for ever and ever. Amen.

A Prayer for the Week:

Purify our conscience, Almighty God, by your daily visitation, that your Son Jesus Christ, at his coming, may find in us a mansion prepared for himself; who lives and reigns with you, in the unity of the Holy Spirit, one God, now and for ever. Amen.

Christmas Eve

Waiting Like Simeon

A
S WE CONCLUDE ADVENT and our exploration this week of how different people in the Scripture's story waited on God, we finish with someone who may seem to be an unlikely candidate to be written about on Christmas Eve. But I do so because he is the first individual described by the gospel writers as someone who waited: an old man named Simeon.[70]

> *Now there was a man in Jerusalem called Simeon, who was righteous and devout. He was waiting for the consolation of Israel, and the Holy Spirit was on him. It had been revealed to him by the Holy Spirit that he would not die before he had seen the Lord's Messiah.*[71]

As with Zechariah, Luke is giving high praise to Simeon through this introduction. He tells us that Simeon was righteous, devout, and in the full passage Luke mentions three times in three verses how the Holy Spirit rested on Simeon, revealed things to him, and guided him. If we want to become people like that, we must consider: What was waiting like for Simeon, and on this Christmas Eve, why does it matter to us?

As we said when we began this Advent, waiting isn't easy. It grates against us. Many times, waiting is not only inconvenient, but involves real pain. It was like that for Simeon—during his decades of waiting, his eyes had probably seen some harrowing and traumatic things. Luke doesn't put a number on Simeon's age, but we get the sense that he was aged.

About 80 years before Jesus' birth, before the Romans were in power in Jerusalem, there had been a civil war and at its end the Hasmonean ruler, Alexander, crucified 800 Jews in Jerusalem for rebelling against him.

Then, around 20 years later, the Romans came with all of their brutality, and through them in another 20 years, Herod. Regardless of what Simeon's exact age was when Luke introduced him to us, his eyes had surely seen plenty of suffering. For Simeon's entire life, pagans dominated and oppressed his people, while he waited, and waited, for the comfort of Israel.

In addition to the things that he saw during his lifetime, we can also be sure that the suffering that predated him also never would have been far from Simeon's mind. Simeon's people, God's people, Israel, had been oppressed for almost six centuries by the time that we learn about Simeon's waiting.

And going back even farther, for much of their history as a people—even when they weren't subject to foreign nations, on another level, they had never really lived up to their covenant with God. They had never been the light to the nations they were intended to be. They had never fully been the righteous and devout nation God called them to be. Simeon, however, was righteous and devout, and he waited. By the time Luke introduces him into the story, not just his own waiting, but the entire history of the waiting of his people would have been etched into the wrinkles on his face and into the eyes that were always looking for the coming of the Messiah.

Even though Simeon is something of an obscure character in the Bible, he's intriguing to me. He isn't one of the main characters in the story, but rather is someone off in the periphery waiting on God throughout a lifetime. Even though we have so little information about him, what Luke does tell us can give us some clues of how Simeon became so open to God during the course of his waiting through a lifetime.

First, Luke's description of him as righteous and devout surely meant that he had a heart inwardly open toward God, but in the ancient Jewish world of Luke and Simeon, it also would have referred to the exterior things he did. He kept the commandments. He participated in the community's rhythm of prayer, worship, fasting, and giving. In other words, he had a lifestyle of holy habits.

Luke clues us into one of those habits for Simeon. Simeon wasn't just a man who read his Scriptures, he drank deeply from them. Through the words that Simeon speaks (which we'll explore tomorrow), we see how the thoughts that he expressed were dripping with the Scriptures he had absorbed over so many years. Luke points us toward that in this introduction by describing Simeon as one who "was waiting for the consolation [or comfort] of Israel." That's another reference to those first words of Isaiah's "book of comfort" we talked about last week with John the Baptist: "Comfort, comfort my people, says your God...," and then it goes on to describe the voice of the one calling in the wilderness to prepare the way of the Lord's coming.

Simeon had ingested the vision of the Scriptures, particularly of Isaiah 40-55, to the point that it had given a framework for everything he was waiting for in his life. It gave context to all of the suffering that his eyes had seen, and it gave hope for those eyes to keep waking up and watching for Israel's true King to come at last.

Christmas Eve is as good a time as any to consider what is giving shape to our lives the way that the Scriptures gave shape to Simeon's. Perhaps our framework is a desire for success, or for comfort, or to be loved. Whatever it is, we will certainly be better prepared to welcome the King if we can identify it and make any necessary changes in light of all that his coming into the world means.

We also see that Simeon listened. Luke tells us that the Holy Spirit communicated things to Simeon about the Messiah. Certainly one way that Simeon listened was by soaking his mind in the Scriptures, as we just described. But I think he did it another way, too: he was probably quiet and listening countless days when the Spirit wasn't saying anything to him about the Messiah. This habit ensured that be attentive whenever the right time would come.

I've mentioned the importance of silence a few times throughout Advent, because I'm convinced we don't have enough of it in our lives. We've got to practice listening to God and sometimes—even many times—that's going to involve quieting ourselves and hearing *nothing* from God. If we don't practice that, we might not be paying any attention when God does want to say something.

So, in light of your Christmas Eve today and your Christmas Day tomorrow, are there any ways in which it would be appropriate for you to be quiet with God as a way of practicing being attentive to him? (And if we aren't attentive to him on *these* holy days, do we really expect the rest of our year to be substantially different?)

Simeon soaked his mind in the Scriptures. Simeon listened quietly to God. And the third thing we can learn about his waiting is that he did those two things for a long time. Simeon didn't just wait on God through the four weeks of Advent. Simeon's Advent had been a lifetime.

May it be so for you and me too, so that we can let the church's call of Advent through the centuries incessantly ring throughout our souls:

Our King and Savior now draws near. Come, let us adore him.

A Prayer for the Day:

O God, you make us glad by the yearly festival of the birth of your only Son Jesus Christ: Grant that we, who joyfully receive him as our Redeemer, may with sure confidence behold him when he comes to be our Judge; who lives and reigns with you and the Holy Spirit, one God, now and for ever. Amen.

Rejoicing Like Simeon

ONE OF THE MOST OVERWHELMING MOMENTS of my life was when I became a father. When I held my newborn son for the first time, I was on the verge of losing all composure. His little eyes were wide open and staring at mine, and the fact that he was there, alive and healthy…I can't put it into words.

There were a lot of factors that went into the emotions I felt that morning when he was born. The delivery had been hard on both my wife and the baby, so holding him knowing that they were both safe and sound was accompanied by a tremendous sense of relief and gratitude. The tension in our waiting for his arrival started before that day, however. Though he was born in Texas, my wife and I had lived in Guatemala for the majority of her pregnancy, and much of that time had not gone smoothly. We lived in a foreign country, and she had been on bed rest for a significant portion of the time (and I didn't know how to cook). There were a lot of days when we were anxious about the survival of our baby.

Even before that, the day that we found out my wife was expecting was an adventure. She was in a Guatemalan emergency room with pneumonia. Just as the staff was getting ready to run some x-rays, her doctor happened to be on duty and said, "let's make sure we can do this." They took some blood, ran the test, and a few minutes later, he answered the phone, then hung it up and said, "Congratulations!" It was an interesting and unexpected beginning to what would be a difficult nine months.

To go back even further: my wife and I were married for six years before she became pregnant. We waited a long time, and we were more excited than we ever had been before when we found out she was expecting. But that pregnancy's result wasn't the baby boy I held in Texas. We never got to hold that baby—the pregnancy ended early in a miscarriage. Our hopes that had built over the years, and which went through the roof when she was expecting, came crashing down with one visit to her doctor when there suddenly was no heartbeat. We were crushed, and our waiting continued.

All of that and more went into the rush of emotions I felt when I held my baby boy that first time. We had waited, and waited painfully, for his arrival. The feeling of the expression that was on my face when he finally entered the world is permanently etched into my memory, and it was full of a lot of waiting, a lot of pain, a lot of hope, and an immense amount of joy.

Since I can still feel the look that was on my face that day, it makes me wonder what Simeon's face looked like when the moment came for which he had spent a lifetime in attentive waiting on God:

Now there was a man in Jerusalem called Simeon, who was righteous and devout. He was waiting for the consolation of Israel, and the Holy Spirit was on him. It had been revealed to him by the Holy Spirit that he would not die before he had seen the Lord's Messiah. Moved by the Spirit, he went into the temple courts. When the parents brought in the child Jesus to do for him what the custom of the Law required, Simeon took him in his arms and praised God, saying:

"Sovereign Lord, as you have promised,
you may now dismiss your servant in peace.
For my eyes have seen your salvation,
which you have prepared in the sight of all nations:

a light for revelation to the Gentiles,
and the glory of your people Israel.'[72]

What was the look on his face that day? How did his face look when the Spirit guided him into the Temple? What was his expression when he saw the peasant couple from Nazareth? What would anyone have thought who saw him as he approached the young family and held out his arms? What was the look on his face when he held that baby for whom he—and in fact all of Israel, and all of the world—had been waiting so long?

Obviously, we don't have a picture of the old man's face on that day, but we do have his words. They're rich words, and they tell us a lot about Simeon, a lot about that baby boy that he held in his arms as he said them, and a lot about how you and I would be wise to live in light of both of their lives.

As we mentioned yesterday, Simeon's waiting was characterized by soaking his mind in the Scriptures, and in this brief prayer we see the part of the Scripture on which he had focused his attention. Again, it's Isaiah 40-55, the "book of comfort," which not only communicates God's compassion on Israel, but it looks forward to the one through whom God's deliverance and comfort would come to his people. It speaks of God's salvation being made evident and visible to all the nations of the world, "a light for the Gentiles, to open eyes that are blind, to free captives from prison and to release from the dungeon those that sit in darkness."[73]

So, when I wonder about the look that would have been on Simeon's face as he rejoiced at the fact that he was holding the newborn Jesus in his arms, I again have to take into account how deeply Simeon had soaked the Scripture's message into his soul. And then, at that moment, when he saw that baby— *the* baby—who by some means God had told him was to be the King of Israel, the King of the world...

...the one who would fulfill Israel's longing for a true heir to David's throne, who would deliver Israel from their oppressors once and for all...

...the one who would fulfill Israel's longing for the Temple, the place where heaven and earth overlapped and interlocked (and even if Simeon couldn't foresee it, Jesus would somehow do so by *being* that heaven-and-earth-place himself)...

...the one who would satisfy Israel's longing for the Torah, as the true King would do, by fulfilling the Torah himself and enabling the people to do so as well...

...the one who would usher in the fulfillment of Israel's longing for new creation, as the King who would finally have the wisdom to bring about the time when everything would be made new and made right...

In thinking about what expression would have been on Simeon's face, I've got to factor in this bubbling up and pouring out of his knowledge of these Scriptures, his faith that they would be fulfilled, and his joy that right there, in that baby whom he held and at whom he surely stared in wide-eyed, open-mouthed wonder...it was all reaching its climax, it was all coming to pass, it was all going to happen—in that infant baby peasant boy.

Simeon had waited, and waited painfully, for that boy's arrival. Finally the day came, and he held the Messiah in his arms. The expression on his face when he did so surely showed a lot of waiting, a lot of pain, a lot of hope, and an immense amount of joy.

If Simeon hadn't waited like he did, he wouldn't have had the overwhelming joy of that day with the infant King in his arms. If we don't wait through Advent, the joy of this day won't be as complete.

But now, we have waited, and he has come, and we should therefore celebrate as if we are people whose every deep longing has been met in a surprising, shocking, instant. Because that is indeed what happened in Bethlehem, what happens every day that you and I abide in him now, and what will happen when he comes again.

Alleluia! To us a child is born:
O come, let us adore him. Alleluia!

See—I am bringing you good news of great joy for all the people: to you is born this day in the city of David a Savior, who is the Messiah, the Lord.[74]

See, the home of God is among mortals.
He will dwell with them;
they will be his peoples,
and God himself will be with them....[75]

A Prayer for the Day:

Almighty God, you have given your only-begotten Son to take our nature upon him, and to be born this day of a pure virgin: Grant that we, who have been born again and made your children by adoption and grace, may daily be renewed by your Holy Spirit; through our Lord Jesus Christ, to whom with you and the same Spirit be honor and glory, now and for ever. Amen.

Traditional Advent Readings

(from the Revised Common Lectionary)

	Old Testament	Psalm	Epistle	Gospel
Year A (2016, 2019, 2022...)				
First Sunday	Is. 2:1-5	Ps. 122	Rom. 13:11-14	Matt. 24:36-44
Second Sunday	Is. 11:1-10	Ps. 72:1-7, 18-19	Rom. 15:4-13	Matt. 3:1-12
Third Sunday	Is. 35:1-10	Luke 1:47-55	James 5:7-10	Matt. 11:2-11
Fourth Sunday	Is. 7:10-16	Ps. 80:1-7, 17-19	Rom. 1:1-7	Matt. 1:18-25
Year B (2014, 2017, 2020...)				
First Sunday	Is. 64:1-9	Ps. 80:1-7, 17-19	1 Cor. 1:3-9	Mark 13:24-37
Second Sunday	Is. 40:1-11	Ps. 85:1-2, 8-13	2 Pet. 3:8-15a	Mark 1:1-8
Third Sunday	Is. 61:1-4, 8-11	Ps. 126	1 Thess. 5:16-24	Jn. 1:6-8, 19-28
Fourth Sunday	2 Sam. 7:1-11,16	Luke 1:47-55	Rom. 16:25-27	Luke 1:26-38

	Old Testament	Psalm	Epistle	Gospel
Year C (2015, 2018, 2021...)				
First Sunday	Jer. 33:14-16	Ps. 25:1-10	1 Thess. 3:9-13	Luke 21:25-36
Second Sunday	Mal. 3:1-4	Luke 1:68-79	Phil. 1:3-11	Luke 3:1-6
Third Sunday	Zeph. 3:14-20	Is. 12:2-6	Phil. 4:4-7	Luke 3:7-18
Fourth Sunday	Micah 5:2-5a	Luke 1:47-55	Heb. 10:5-10	Luke 1:39-45

Appendix B

How to Spend a Day
Alone with God

When we mention solitude and attempt to commit ourselves to it, a push/pull phenomenon almost always comes into play. We long for time alone with God, but we also resist it at multiple levels. That resistance most often surfaces in the form of thinking that we have too much to do to take a day away, but the real issue(s) are probably deeper than that. Solitude opens up the space for God to deal with things at some of those other levels which we are normally very good at ignoring.

As for details on how to go about this and what to do, please feel free to do it in a way that suits you and your life with your family. The point is to do it, not to do it perfectly.

For example, some people may be able to take a full twenty-four hour period and get away. Normally, for my wife and me, our day in solitude ends up being the length of a work day so that we can be back home with our children for the evening. Find the length of time that works best for you.

As for the arrangement and content of the day, I would encourage you simply to try not to fill it with much. You'll want to unplug from technology and be reasonably inaccessible. I find that I can't spend days like this in my own house, but my wife can. It's fine to have something to read—certainly some Scripture and perhaps one other book, but even these can be twisted into tools we use to avoid God in solitude rather than encounter him. So, make use of them as you wish, but without using them to cram full the space in the day that has been opened up for you and God. Journaling is good if it is a habit for you, or even if it feels inviting to you. But the bottom line is that there are no demands on you for this day—just be with God.

You might come away from a day like this encouraged and refreshed, or you might feel plain bored. Don't be concerned with whether you "did" it well or poorly. The issue is more about having a day in which we let everything else go in order to be with our Friend. You may find it helpful to keep in mind the simple question, "What would God and I like to do together today?"

For years, I wanted to have days like this, but virtually never took them. I felt like they were a luxury and the demands of a life in ministry were too much for me to afford them. In that regard, I was badly educated, or—more likely—self-deceived. Now I view them as an indispensable part of the kind of life and ministry I want to have.[76]

Notes

[1] This is an abbreviated version of Dallas Willard's definition of joy: "Joy is not pleasure, a mere sensation, but a pervasive and constant sense of wellbeing. It claims our entire body and soul, both the physical and the non-physical side of the human self. Hope in the goodness of God is joy's indispensable support." From http://www.dwillard.org/resources/WillardWords.asp, accessed September 17, 2014.

[2] Ruth Haley Barton, *2013 Advent Reflections*.

[3] John Wesley, Sermon 16, "The Means of Grace," in *The Sermons of John Wesley*, ed. Thomas Jackson, The Wesley Center Online, accessed October 23, 2014, http://wesley.nnu.edu/john-wesley/the-sermons-of-john-wesley-1872-edition/sermon-16-the-means-of-grace/

[4] Danny E. Morris and Charles M. Olsen, *Discerning God's Will Together: A Spiritual Practice for the Church* (Nashville: Upper Room Books, 1997) Kindle Edition, Location 1273.

[5] Richard J. Foster, *Prayer: Finding the Heart's True Home* (New York: HarperCollins, 1992) 9.

[6] James Bryan Smith, *The Good and Beautiful Life: Putting on the Character of Christ* (Downers Grove, Ill: InterVarsity Press, 2009) 183-184.

[7] Wesley, "Means of Grace"

[8] Willard states, "You may have been told that it is good to read the Bible through every year and that you can ensure this will happen by reading so many verses per day from the Old and New Testaments. If you do this you may enjoy the reputation of one who reads the Bible through each year, and you may congratulate yourself on it. But will you become more like Christ and more filled with the life of God?...It is better in one year to have ten good verses transferred into the substance of our lives than to have every word of the Bible flash before our eyes."
Dallas Willard, *Hearing God: Developing a Conversational Relationship with God,* (Downers Grove, Ill.: InterVarsity Press, 1999), 163.

[9] M. Robert Mulholland Jr., *Shaped by the Word: The Power of Scripture in Spiritual Formation,* (Nashville: Upper Room Books, 1985), 39-41.

[10] Hebrews 4:12-13

[11] Wesley, "Means of Grace"

[12] Matthew 26:29

[13] Dallas Willard, *The Spirit of the Disciplines: Understanding How God Changes Lives*, (New York: HarperCollins, 1988) 101.

[14] Ibid. 107-108

[15] "Worst Christian Book Covers of 2012," *Englewood Review of Books*, http://erb.kingdomnow.org/worst-christian-book-covers-of-2012/12/, accessed September 17, 2014

[16] Though I have chosen not to delve into deconstructing these interpretations of Scripture in this series, good resources are available to help anyone who wants to examine them in further detail. I have been most influenced by the writings of New Testament scholar N.T. Wright whose *For Everyone* series of commentaries on the entire New Testament is remarkably readable and helpful.

[17] Maltbie D. Babcock, "This is My Father's World," Public Domain, 1901.

[18] See N.T. Wright, *Surprised by Hope: Rethinking Heaven, the Resurrection, and the Mission of the Church,* (New York: HarperCollins, 2008).

[19] N.T. Wright, *Revelation for Everyone* (Louisville: Westminster John Knox Press, 2011), 224-225.

[20] James Bryan Smith, *The Good and Beautiful God: Falling in Love with the God Jesus Knows* (Downers Grove, Ill: InterVarsity Press, 2009), 124-125.

[21] "Preface to Advent" from *The Book of Common Prayer*.

[22] Dallas Willard, *The Divine Conspiracy: Rediscovering Our Hidden Life in God* (New York: HarperCollins, 1997), 399.

[23] N.T. Wright, *Simply Christian: Why Christianity Makes Sense* (New York: HarperCollins, 2006), 217, 219.

[24] 1 Corinthians 15:58

[25] N.T. Wright, *Paul for Everyone: 1 Corinthians* (Louisville: Westminster John Knox Press, 2003) 227-228.

[26] Though I've communicated it in my own way, virtually everything I say in this post I learned from N.T. Wright, especially through his commentary on Matthew 1:1-17 in *Matthew for Everyone*.

[27] N.T. Wright, *Matthew for Everyone* (Louisville: Westminster John Knox Press, 2002), 3.

[28] See Wright's glossary entry for *Messiah* in *Matthew for Everyone*: "The Hebrew word means literally 'anointed one,' hence in theory either a prophet, priest, or king. In Greek this translates as Christos; 'Christ' in early Christianity was a title, and only gradually became an alternative proper name for Jesus. In practice, 'Messiah' is mostly restricted to the notion, which took various forms in ancient Judaism, of the coming king who would be David's true heir, through whom YHWH would rescue Israel from pagan enemies. There was no single template of expectations. Scriptural stories and promises contributed to different ideals and movements, often focused on (a) decisive military defeat of Israel's enemies and (b) rebuilding or cleansing the Temple...." (215).

[29] Again, much of what I say here is heavily informed by the writings of N.T. Wright. For more on today's topic, see Chapter Six ("Israel") of *Simply Christian: Why Christianity Makes Sense* (New York, HarperCollins, 2006.

[30] Wright, *Simply Christian*, 64-65.

[31] Psalm 79:1-5a

[32] Wright, *Simply Christian*, 81-82.

[33] Ibid. 82.

[34] Isaiah 2:4

[35] Isaiah 35:1,5-7a,10

[36] Isaiah 64:1a,6-9

[37] Isaiah 65:17-25

[38] Wright, *Simply Christian*, 84.

[39] Isaiah 11:2-4a,6,9

[40] Luke 3:2b-6

[41] Isaiah 40:1-3

[42] Habakkuk 1:2

[43] Habakkuk 2:1

[44] Habakkuk 2:20

[45] Psalm 13:1-2

[46] Psalm 74:10

[47] Psalm 90:13

[48] Psalm 119:84

[49] Luke 1:5-7

[50] See N.T. Wright, *Luke for Everyone*, 19.

[51] Luke 1:67-79

[52] Wright, *Luke for Everyone*, 8.

[53] See Luke 1:73.

[54] See Luke 1:55.

[55] Victor P. Hamilton, *Handbook on the Pentateuch* (Grand Rapids, MI: Baker Book House, 1982), 95-96.

[56] John 8:56-59

[57] Psalm 77:20

[58] 2 Samuel 7:8,16

[59] Psalm 80:1a,2b-3

[60] John 10:11

[61] John 21:16

[62] John 1:29

[63] Hebrews 13:20

[64] Revelation 7:17

[65] Robert C. Pelfrey, *Rock God: How God Shakes, Rattles and Rolls our Easy-Listening Lives* (Midland, TX: SalvationLife Books, 2014), 15.

[66] John 10:14-16

[67] Wright, *Luke for Everyone*. 12.

[68] Luke 1:46-55

[69] 1 Samuel 2:1,5,7-8

[70] Much of the content of this entry was influenced by the chapter titled "Simeon's Song" in Jack Levison's outstanding book, *Fresh Air: The Holy Spirit for an Inspired Life* (Brewster, Mass: Paraclete Press, 2012).

[71] Luke 2:25-26, NIV

[72] Luke 2:25-32

[73] Isaiah 42:6b-7, NIV

[74] Luke 2:10-11

[75] Revelation 21:3

[76] Adapted from Daniel Ethan Harris, "How to Spend a Day Alone with God," *SalvationLife* (blog), Nov. 26, 2013, http://www.salvationlife.com/blog/2013/11/26/how-to-spend-a-day-alone-with-god.

44203736R00083

Made in the USA
San Bernardino, CA
09 January 2017

Made in the USA
Monee, IL
07 October 2022

15404457R00135